THE NEW MANAGER PLAYBOOK

A Simple Guide for Leading with Ease

LIA GARVIN

Love for *The New Manager Playbook*:

"*The New Manager Playbook* is an essential guide that empowers new leaders to navigate the exhilarating yet daunting transition into management. As the founder of Drybar, I understand the challenges firsthand, and Lia's journey offers invaluable insights drawn from her decade of experience at companies like Microsoft, Apple, and Google. This book feels like a heart-to-heart with a mentor, helping you build trust, master conflict resolution, and forge deep connections with your team. Emphasizing the human side of leadership, it provides practical strategies to create a thriving environment for all. Lia is a thoughtful leader, and this book is a blessing to our world—get ready to dive in and transform your approach to management!"

—Alli Webb, Founder of Drybar

"*The New Manager Playbook* is an insightful guide to help provide new managers with the tools they need to excel. Garvin's approach is both encouraging and realistic, empowering the reader to navigate the challenges of management. Through a combination of personal anecdotes, real-world examples, and actionable advice, Garvin breaks down essential skills such as setting expectations, giving feedback, delegating effectively, and fostering accountability. What sets this book apart is its emphasis on building trust and fostering genuine relationships within a team. Garvin advocates for a 'results-based relationship' model, akin to a sports team, where mutual respect and a shared commitment to success drive performance. This approach not only encourages a healthy work dynamic but also empowers team members to take ownership of their work and contribute their best efforts. Overall, *The New Manager Playbook* is an invaluable asset for first-time managers seeking to cultivate a thriving and motivated team while developing their own leadership capabilities."

—Rajan Patel, VP of Search, Google

"As a design leader, it's crucial to guide your team through ambiguity. *The New Manager Playbook* offers valuable insights for all leaders, particularly emphasizing the significance of active listening to comprehend challenges and foster empathy, especially during times of change and uncertainty. This book provides practical advice on empowering teams to navigate complex situations and to deliver success together."

—Albert Shum, former CVP of Design at Microsoft

"Garvin's insights from her years in team operations at top tech companies make this book an invaluable resource for new managers. Her strategies for building resilient, high-performing teams are both practical and forward-thinking. This playbook is recommended reading for anyone looking to excel in a leadership role."

—Joshua To, VP of Design, Meta

"Lia Garvin's decade of experience at tech giants like Microsoft, Apple, and Google shines through in this essential guide for new managers. Her practical strategies for building trust, **resolving conflicts, and motivating teams** are invaluable, and I've personally seen her apply these strategies with great success. *The New Manager Playbook* is a must-read for anyone stepping into a leadership role."

—Carla H. McIntosh, former VP of Talent Acquisition at Reddit

"Being a new manager can be one of the most overwhelming times in your career, and most of us were initially thrown into it with barely any tools in our toolboxes. You want to do your best but it takes time to learn the balance of delegating more and micromanaging less for the growth of your team. *The New Manager Playbook* is the guide that any new manager needs to not only feel confident managing their team, but in doing the necessary steps to supporting their team in reaching their full potential. It is a fun read, full of practical and actionable tools that will help any new manager go from good to great."

—Shelby Rhodes, Chief of Staff to the CEO, Strava

"Management is often something that happens to you, not something you plan for or choose – at least it was in my case. I wish I'd had something like *The New Manager Playbook* back then. It's a reliable companion that offers expert guidance, relatable examples, and proven strategies to help you lead with empathy, set clear expectations, and achieve outstanding results."

– Jonathan Terleski, Head of Design, YouTube

THE NEW MANAGER PLAYBOOK

A Simple Guide for Leading with Ease

LIA GARVIN

Copyright © 2025- Reflek Publishing

All Rights Reserved.

No part of this publication may be reproduced, distributed, or transmitted in any form or by any means, including photocopying, recording, or other electronic or mechanical methods, without the prior written permission of the publisher, except in the case of brief quotations embodied in critical reviews and certain other noncommercial uses permitted by copyright law.

Disclaimer: The author makes no guarantees concerning the level of success you may experience by following the advice and strategies contained in this book, and you accept the risk that results will differ for each individual. The purpose of this book is to educate, entertain, and inspire.

For more information: hello@liagarvin.com

ISBN PAPERBACK: 978-1-962280-73-0
ISBN EBOOK: 978-1-962280-74-7

Dedication

To first-time managers: I promise it gets easier.

Table of Contents

Chapter 1: The Complexities of Being a Manager
The power, the responsibility, and everything in between 11

Chapter 2: Setting an Intention for Success
Can I do this? Should I do this? Do I even want to do this? 33

Chapter 3: Establishing Mutual Trust
What's trust got to do with it? Oh everything? Cool. 51

Chapter 4: Getting to Know Your Team
Building a results-based relationship 71

Chapter 5: Bringing Out the Best in Our Teams
Setting expectations, giving useful feedback,
and making accountability not scary.. 93

Chapter 6: Freeing Up Time to Truly Lead
Unlocking the secrets to delegating, coaching,
and not trying to do everything ourselves................................ 123

Chapter 7: Motivating Your Team to Excel
And can we not advertise how little work we're doing? 145

Chapter 8: Conflict Management
Navigating the stickiest situations…of which there are many 157

Chapter 9: Hiring and Onboarding
Expanding your team thoughtfully 173

Conclusion 191
Acknowledgments... 197
Help spread the word! 199
Endnotes 201

"PEOPLE LEAVE MANAGERS, NOT COMPANIES."

—Marcus Buckingham,
Author and Cocreator
of StrengthsFinder

Chapter 1
The Complexities of Being a Manager

The power, the responsibility, and everything in between

I always wanted to be a manager—growing a team, being a leader, helping people reach their full potential.

That is, until I took on my first role as a manager, when I realized the whole thing was *way* harder than anyone ever tells you.

Which brings me to Paul.

Paul and I were peers when I joined the team, and we were told we'd each be responsible for different areas of the work. But after I joined, it quickly became clear that Paul was barely doing any work. To make matters worse, he had been causing tension with our partner teams—talking over people, making jokes at the wrong times, and acting like he was the most important person in every room.

Even so, Paul and I had a good rapport as peers, and when I was asked to be his manager, I said, "Of course," without thinking twice.

As a fixer, I was used to being parachuted into a sticky situation and turning things around to operate seamlessly within weeks. But let's be honest: no one wants to be treated like a project. And no one wants to feel like they've been passed up for an opportunity they'd been waiting for. Unbeknownst to me, as a substitute for giving Paul any semblance of performance feedback, our shared manager had told him long before I joined the team that *Paul* would become the manager. When it was announced that I would be the manager, the rapport Paul and I had built quickly turned cold, with a particularly icy interaction when he claimed I stole his job.

I understood his frustration. I've been there: you are on the team for a long time, people are sending you positive signals, and then out of nowhere, someone new joins, and it feels like you got the rug pulled out from under you.

But navigating this as a first-time manager was overwhelming to say the least. With an uncomfortable dynamic established from day one of my new role, it certainly didn't feel like I was "in charge" of anything.

Was I supposed to give feedback about the frustrations *other teams* were having with Paul? How much should I follow up with him if work that he was supposed to be doing *wasn't* getting done? Did I still have to talk to him when he made it clear he wasn't interested in talking to *me*?

Paul's performance, or lack thereof, spoke for itself. After I absorbed his workload because nothing was getting done, my manager took the reins and moved Paul to another division in the company.

My first foray into managing was going GREAT.

Next, there was Mindy.

Mindy joined the team I was on years later at a different company. We were peers and immediately became friends. We had lunch together every day, hung out on the weekends, and shared all of the office gossip. When I went on maternity leave, she and I met for lunch almost weekly so that she could keep me up to speed with the happenings on the team, and neither of us could wait for my return.

When I came back from maternity leave, I was promoted and asked to be Mindy's manager. Unlike Paul, Mindy was excited about the change and the opportunity it might create for her since we were such good friends.

Even though this arrangement had a much better chance of success than managing Paul did, at the time I was unaware that having a personal relationship does *not* solve everything. In fact, it makes things more complicated. Mindy and I never talked about what the management change would mean for our relationship, and it was all sunshine and roses until, well, it wasn't.

Mindy was fantastic at event planning and took on the task of planning a major event for our team. This was in her wheelhouse and offered a great opportunity for her to really lead a project, end to end. At first it went really well—she came up with cool, outside-the-box ideas and was building a lot of buzz for the event.

But she was also planning another event at the same time: her wedding.

Her own big day was justifiably more important to Mindy. It was not, however, to the VP of our team.

In the weeks leading up to the wedding, Mindy was nowhere to be found. She left for appointments that lasted more than half the day, went radio silent on communicating progress regarding time-sensitive deadlines, and worked from home on days she was supposed to be in the office to review elements of the event—and this was long before COVID made working from home routine.

As her friend, I understood she had a lot going on. But as her manager, I was thinking, *What the actual f*ck dude? Don't do this to me.* I felt conflicted—and, honestly, disrespected. I'll talk later in the book about how to handle the shift from being a peer or friend into a manager with direct report, but for now, let's just say I didn't handle it in the way I will recommend to you.

I gave feedback; it got tense. One afternoon in a team meeting, I asked Mindy to give an update on the status of some of the final arrangements for the event, and she said I was talking down to her. She then filed an HR complaint. Terrified that an HR complaint was synonymous with being arrested, I followed up with HR to see if I should start packing my belongings. They replied that a manager asking for the status of a project is *not,* in fact, an HR violation and I should continue giving her feedback directly if her performance was lacking.

Cool. Yeah, I could do that, or…I could quit being a manager altogether. The latter option seemed a lot more appealing.

Chapter 1

I begged my manager to not make me manage Mindy anymore, but she told me to "stick with it." BRUTAL.

Eventually, through some more tools I'll share with you in this book, we resolved our issues. As luck would have it, my manager eventually restructured the team and moved Mindy to another manager, but let's just say of experience number two: WORSE.

Then there was Shariah, where everything I'd learned came together.

The amazingness of this woman deserves to be shouted from the rooftops. This is why managing is such an emotional rollercoaster: because when you do get a great team member, you love every moment of being their manager.

Shariah joined my team to take over the role I had been doing before I became a manager. This is a really difficult situation for someone to enter into, and Shariah crushed it. She was respectful of the foundation I'd laid, brought amazing ideas for how to elevate the work, and was hungry for feedback and to develop her skills.

Shariah helped me find my groove as a leader. Working with her taught me the importance of giving someone the space to rise to their full potential, not worrying about holding too tightly to control everything because you see the "rising tides lifts all boats" situation unfolding in real time.

Whenever I'd meet with anyone she was working with, people would commend me on finding such an awesome person for the team, eager to share a story about something she had helped them with. She reenergized my love for managing people and ignited my spark of encouraging people stick with it, even when it's hard.

Why We're Here

We've all heard the quote that opened this chapter—"people leave managers, not companies"[1]—and have probably even experienced leaving a role because of a bad manager. Maybe more than once.

Even if you've been blessed with the good fortune of having only fantastic managers, in the *State of the American Manager Report,* the Gallup organization found that *half* of employees report leaving a job because of a bad manager.[2]

So my question to you is this: Do you want to be the manager of the team where people are staying, or of the team where people are leaving?

I wrote this book because I know that managers like you want to *lower* the percentage of people who leave. There will always be some employee turnover for a multitude of factors: changing interests, desiring responsibilities different from what the company can offer, pivoting careers, evolving family needs. But the primary reason does not have to be because of a bad manager.

What constitutes a bad manager?

Here are a few core characteristics: micromanagement, unclear priorities, lack of meaningful feedback, lack of recognition, inability to motivate, and poor communication skills. It's no coincidence that a bad manager lacks the exact skills we're going to talk about in this book.

No one is a bad manager on purpose. The reality is, we simply don't always think about all the things that go into being a *good* manager. Or we do think about them, run into some hiccups, get overwhelmed, and then project that stress back onto our teams.

But it's not just our teams who are suffering.

Here's the second reason we're here: as managers, we are burning out.

Microsoft's 2023 *Work Trend Index Report*, based on interviews with more than twenty thousand people, found that 53 percent of managers report feeling burned out.[3] That's a greater percentage than among employees, who come in a close second at 48 percent. So basically, we're all feeling pretty fried.

In my own firsthand experience as a manager—as well as what I've gathered from the managers I've trained and coached—one of the biggest sources of burnout is that managing can feel as if you're a diamond stuck in a lump of coal being squeezed from all directions. From one angle, you have your teams relying on you to know everything and have it all figured out, even when things are constantly changing. From another, your own management chain is pressuring you to get work done faster. From another, you have partner teams to collaborate with or rely on who don't always meet their deadlines. And from another, there are clients or stakeholders from other parts of the company who bring their own sets of demands. Challenges come at you from all angles, and as a new manager, you likely don't feel equipped to handle all of them.

Hybrid and distributed work has introduced new complexities with communication. Economic pressures require us to do more work with less staff, less time, and less money. The competitive landscape in many industries requires us to move faster and make quicker pivots, which can lead to disconnects and confusion around priorities. Managers who aren't equipped to deal with these pressures—which new managers naturally don't feel that comfortable doing right out of the gate—often contribute to the communication gaps or inconsistencies that make all of this work harder.

I'm not blaming you. You are not responsible for the lack of training and support given to most managers starting in the role. You're being asked to take on more responsibilities, often while still carrying many of your previous responsibilities, and are just expected to figure it out.

It isn't fair. You likely have not been set up for success.

But the awesome thing is you are still NEW AT IT. Unlike so many managers in the past, *you* have a playbook to help you learn and practice the fundamental skills of effective management so that you don't have to figure everything out as you go.

You get to start on a new path, one where very early in your tenure as a manager, you can feel confident that you are good at it, that you are adding value, and that your team benefits from the work you invest your time and energy into.

With awareness, intention, training, and support, *everyone* has the potential to become a great manager.

Chapter 1

The fact that you have picked up this book shows you are interested in getting better at managing. Now it's time to learn and internalize the tools and skills that will help you reach that potential.

Let's start today.

I'm here to be your own personal team whisperer to help you every step of the way. I do things a little differently from some of the books you might have read or trainings you've attended. I don't just talk theory without action. And I don't paint a rosy picture where there isn't one. Instead of feeling like someone is talking *at* you, I want you to feel like someone is locking arms *with* you—or if that feels too cheesy, sitting down for a beer with you.

This whole "feeling in over your head" thing doesn't have to keep you up all night anymore. (We'll let the hangxiety from the beers do that.)

The Stakes Are High

In my workshops and trainings for managers, I often share the famous quote from *Spider-Man*, said by Uncle Ben about Spidey's superpowers: "With great power comes great responsibility."

Managing comes with a great deal of power. Your input guides your team members' salaries and advancement paths. Your input informs the kinds of projects they work on and visibility they get. Your skill level at feedback, delegating, and coaching informs how they work through areas where they're stuck and learn to step up as proactive problem solvers.

You are responsible for helping your teams reach their full potential. You are *not* responsible for doing their job for them or clearing every single obstacle. Instead, you are there to guide, coach, and, most of all, lead them to reach the goals they have for themselves—provided they meet you halfway by doing the work.

You are also responsible for looking beyond your identity, preferences, and personal work style to be empathetic and tuned in to those of the people on your team.

While facilitating a manager development program at a large financial institution a few years ago, I found insights that my client shared from their annual employee engagement survey really eye-opening. One of the lower scoring areas in the survey was people's understanding of the company's benefits. When they dug in deeper, they found that women with women managers were made more aware of the parental leave benefits than the women whose managers were men.

Not pointing any fingers here, but just because *you personally* aren't going to be taking maternity leave doesn't mean you shouldn't understand and communicate the benefits to everyone. I've seen similar issues with managers who were not from underrepresented backgrounds forgetting to communicate about programming being offered to folks from those backgrounds. As a manager, it's your job to understand *all* benefits, accommodations, resources, and programming, regardless of whether you are or will ever be a part of a particular group.

I don't want to sugarcoat the fact that dealing with people involves a lot of complexities, making it an even bigger responsibility to get your job right.

Let's quickly talk through some complexities to be mindful of. The tool to navigate the majority of them is direct communication—being conscious of where you might be generalizing or approaching an interaction with unconscious bias. Instead of generalizing, have a conversation. Consider how you can be more aware of where you've favored your work style at the expense of setting expectations. The following is a sampling and by no means an exhaustive list:

- **Generational Differences**
  The current workforce is composed of four generations—baby boomers, Gen X, millennials, and Gen Z—each with potentially different worldviews, communication styles, work styles, and relationships with time and money. There are lessons to be learned from each generation, and facilitating collaborations across these groups can be a great way to break down the biases and generalizations folks make about each other.

- **Life Stages**
  Be mindful of folks who might be new parents, wrestling with fertility issues, caring for aging parents, or going through perimenopause or menopause, among a number of other potential life stages. For example, research in the journal *Occupational Medicine* cites common menopause symptoms as fatigue, difficulty sleeping, poor concentration, and poor memory, all of which can impact work performance.[4] Perimenopause and menopause are issues very few people are talking about and supporting their employees through, even though they will impact all women employees at some point.

- **Parenting**
  Full disclosure: Before I had kids, I thought parents were exaggerating when they said their kid was sick or had a cold and had to miss school so frequently. Like *every* freaking week? Seemed a little fishy. NOT FISHY. Especially since COVID-19, schools are super strict about when kids can and cannot come to school, leaving parents high and dry with no notice if their kid wakes up with a sniffle. Baby that doesn't sleep, angsty teenager broke curfew and you spend all night pacing around the front door, sixth grader who reminds you at 9 p.m. that they have a science poster due at school by 8 a.m. the next day, and you find yourself at the dining room table until 1 a.m. swearing at a glue stick—all can contribute to a lack of sleep that can impact job performance the next morning.

- **Caregivers**
  We can't assume that people without kids don't have caretaking responsibilities. Many are going through similar challenges of dealing with illness, supporting folks at all hours, or traveling long distances to care for others.

- **Illness**
  People also might be caring for themselves through illnesses that we are not aware of. For example, I have had colleagues wrestling with endometriosis, multiple sclerosis, chronic migraines, and concussions, to name a few. These conditions required long doctor's visits for treatments, downtime for recovery, and the need for other kinds of accommodations.

Chapter 1

- **Geography**
  The Culture Map by Erin Meyer examines the differences in communication style (direct versus indirect) that show up depending on the country you are living in or where you grew up.[5] While there is of course variance within each country and communication style, patterns emerge when it comes to how people navigate conflict, feedback, negotiation, and other issues. These differences are particularly likely to come to a head if you are managing a global team. It's important to get to know each team member and their communication style, as well as that of your own managers, so you can communicate and influence effectively up and down the chain.

- **Location**
  For most workplaces pre-COVID, working in the office was the norm, with some exceptions for occasionally working from home. Now, for many of us, *hybrid* is the norm. Let's be honest: it *is* easier to get a quick sense of what someone is working on when you sit right next to them or can catch them and ask a quick question at the watercooler. For managers of hybrid or distributed teams, not being able to see everyone every day can present challenges for giving feedback, building trust, developing rapport, and reducing micromanagement.

- **Digital Communication**
  Digital communication styles are causing more and more misunderstandings these days. Set norms with your team for when to use email versus chat versus meetings, have conversations about your communication styles, and get ahead of frustrations that show up when someone responds

to a nine-paragraph monologue with the one-word answer "k". Erica Dhawan's book *Digital Body Language* dives into this subject at great length, offering strategies for building connections even when you're communicating mostly asynchronously.[6]

- **Neurodivergence**
  Examples of neurodivergence include having ADHD or dyslexia or being on the autism spectrum. Making reasonable accommodations might result in modified workloads, modified deadlines, or modified but equitable expectations for someone's role.

- **Identity**
  There are eight core dimensions of identity: age, ability, ethnicity, gender, religion, sexual orientation, and socioeconomic status. As managers, it's important to be mindful of where we might be overlooking a need, introducing a bias, or putting someone at a disadvantage because of one of these dimensions. For example, are you avoiding giving feedback to a woman employee that you would freely share with a man employee because you are worried it will hurt her feelings? Have you inadvertently scheduled a team lunch during Ramadan when one of your team members can't participate in eating the meal? Did you schedule a lavish holiday party where someone might not be able to afford a piece of clothing to fit in with the suggested attire?

- **Intersectionality**
  We are all made up of multiple dimensions of the eight identities at the same time (for example, race, age, and

gender). Understanding that our team members might experience multiple layers of adversity because of their intersecting identities helps us show up with more empathy and compassion for our teams and better set people up for success.

There are a wealth of books that give managers a deeper understanding of the different dimensions of identity and how they impact our team members' experiences in the workplace, and help us challenge the assumptions and biases we might be bringing to a situation based on our own experiences. Authors include Daisy Auger-Dominguez, Lily Zheng, Jennifer Brown, Ta-Nehisi Coates, to name a few.

The takeaway? We are all different! That is beautiful and amazing, and mountains of research shows the more diverse a team, the better the results it delivers. That diversity also means not everyone will communicate in the same way or need the same thing from their manager.

I don't list these considerations to scare you—quite the opposite. I share them so that you are prepared. Understanding these differences, and the countless others that I haven't named, will help you be more ready to effectively manage people from all walks of life.

My Commitment to You

In this book, we'll talk about the good, the bad, and the ugly of being a manager—because I assure you that in your management career, you'll experience all three at some point. However, I believe we have the power to make some of the bad and the ugly a little better when we approach managing methodically, intentionally, and compassionately.

Managing is a skill we have to train for. We don't automatically know how to manage just because we're humans living on planet Earth and have talked to other humans before. We don't automatically know how to manage just because we've coached our kid's Little League team that did really well or we were the president of a club, fraternity, or sorority.

Managing people is different. Money is on the line. Careers are on the line. People's professional identities and self-worth can be on the line.

We don't get better at this skill by winging it.

It's something we *always* have to be working on. Doesn't matter if you've heard of some of these concepts already, tried them, or even gotten really freakin' good at them.

A reorg, an acquisition, a pandemic sending everyone into their homes to work remotely, a new generation entering the workforce with a completely different relationship to money and purpose, a deeper integration of technology like AI, a more distributed workforce over more time zones and geographic regions—I could go on, but the point is so much is new. So much is changing.

Despite all the changes, you don't have to be in the dark about the tools at your disposal for navigating these kinds of situations. There is never a one-size-fits-all solution. Being good at managing will require deploying a variety of tools in a myriad of ways, refining

Chapter 1

them as you get more experience under your belt. Your willingness to reflect, learn, and adapt will determine your level of success.

I am so grateful that you've trusted me to hold the torch and light the path through the winding, cavernous tunnel that is first-time managing. Tunnel, cave, rollercoaster, wild ride—use whatever analogy you want for a complicated thing with ups and downs and highs and lows.

From here on out, you don't have to wing it or figure it out alone. And you don't have to subscribe to the false belief that you're the only one who finds managing tough. Trust me: if you are dealing with a problem, someone else has dealt with the exact same thing before or is dealing with it right now.

Having spent a decade driving team operations within companies like Bank of America, Microsoft, Apple, and Google, I've always focused on making it easier for people to get their work done. Now, as a consultant engaging with companies from the outside in, my goal is to make managing the easiest part of work.

This is the book I wish I'd had when I started. Mistakes are part of the job. The point isn't to fear them or avoid them; it's to equip ourselves with the tools to handle them. Provided you put into practice all of what I'll talk about in this book, your job will get easier.

And you know what's kind of cool? The same challenges and themes emerge no matter which industries folks come from. People are people. There are some fundamentals around managing that, when we get them right, allow us to tap into our teams' full potential, reduce burnout, and foster a sense of purpose.

So exciting, right?

That's what gets me out of bed every morning: the idea that we can all have a better manager, someone who motivates instead of micromanaging, leads instead of nitpicking, and amplifies our greatness instead of feeling threatened by it.

We've all had those managers who have made us want to give up. Let's become managers who make our teams want to give their all.

How We'll Get There

Each chapter will focus on a specific topic relevant to managing your team, talk about where it's easy to get stuck, suggest what to try instead, and uncover why this approach is so important.

I've intentionally called this book a *playbook* because it's meant to give play-by-play instructions to deal with the stickiest of situations, paired with tools and exercises. I also include links to worksheets and templates for you to download, routinely updating them to keep the content fresh.

Now I'm not gonna say I always stop what I'm doing to try out the exercises and tools an author links to in their book, but given that this is called a *playbook*, I encourage you to be the better person and do them.

The goal is for you to not only read about some of these concepts but also practice them *before* you enter the battlefield, so you can rely on your muscle memory instead of just hopes, dreams, and fairy dust.

We'll start by talking about the importance of setting an intention as a manager so that you approach the role with a perspective on how you want to show up as a leader, instead of just winging it and continually beating yourself up by wondering, *Really, THAT was the best I could come up with in that situation?*

Then we'll talk about the importance of establishing mutual trust with your team members, both motivating them to do better work and making management tasks like delegating more effortless.

From there, we'll dive into how to build a relationship with your team members, one in which you understand their career goals and aspirations and can help them step into their full potential.

With the foundation of trust and a solid relationship, we'll cover some of the brass tacks—setting expectations, giving feedback, and ensuring accountability—the fundamentals for your team not only to be effective but also to deliver great results.

When you have an accountable team, *they* solve the problems so that all the work doesn't depend on you. With these fundamentals in place, we'll dive into delegating and coaching as two additional power tools in your kit.

But you can't have a high-performing team if motivation is waning, so we'll cover how to keep your team motivated and engaged even amid change, uncertainty, and people just feeling tired of doing their day jobs.

Next is a little party bag of all of the odds and ends that can cause conflict on a team. From my favorite subject and yours, managing former friends, to everyone's worst fear, managing someone with more experience than they have, the penultimate chapter is about how to handle sticky, conflict-laden situations and come away relatively unscathed.

Last but not least, what should you do when you have to expand your team? I've got you covered. I'll close by talking about the fundamentals of hiring effectively and how to onboard team members so they are set up for success even before they start.

A Quick Note before We Dive In

This is a playbook for new managers, meaning my goal is to provide the brass tacks, especially when it comes to the tools and frameworks that I share. If you've been doing your homework leading up to taking on the role of a manager, you will likely have heard about a lot of the tools I talk about.

That's a good thing.

This book isn't about sharing a bunch of frameworks no one has ever heard of before; it's about giving you insights into why we sometimes get stuck and fall short, even when we're using all the right tools—and what to try instead. If you reach a chapter and feel like you've got that skill down already, I encourage you to read it and refresh your understanding of the subject anyway.

None of this work is stuff you learn, file away, and never think about again. Remember all those complexities I talked about? Yeah. As humans, we are continually evolving and changing, and we're always being put to the test.

Chapter 1

You might be great at building rapport with your team, but then a member of your team who is older than you are joins and thinks you don't know what you're doing, and all of your classic moves start falling short.

Being a great manager isn't about knowing what to do in your head; it's about *actually applying* the skills.

With that said, let's get to work.

"ANYTHING DONE WELL STARTS WITH INTENTION, ESPECIALLY IN LEADERSHIP. SET YOUR INTENTION, COMMUNICATE IT ACROSS YOUR TEAM, AND MODEL FOR OTHERS WHAT IT MEANS TO SET, ALIGN, AND EXECUTE AGAINST YOUR INTENTION(S). FROM THERE, THERE'S NO LIMIT TO THE POSSIBILITIES!"

—Farah Bernier,
Vice President of Human Resources at Disney

Chapter 2
Setting an Intention for Success

Can I do this? Should I do this? Do I even want to do this?

"I just want my team to listen to me," Kate said, tearing up. "I want them to respect me because I'm in charge, and still like me as a friend. I also want them to do what I'm asking of them as their boss. But I want them to know they can feel comfortable coming to me for anything."

Kate was all over the place.

She had been asked to be the manager of her team because she was a top performer, but she was immediately flooded with impostor syndrome because she had never managed people before. She had been peers with this group of people for two years, and in wanting to maintain her friendships and be liked, she struggled to establish her authority as a leader.

Kate's sticking points weren't only the facts that she was a new leader and had to reestablish relationships with people she'd known for a while. Instead, because she had not received training on what it meant to be a manager or any support before she started the job, all the things she wanted from being a manager were about how people perceived *her*, not about how to lead her team.

Kate's situation wasn't unique.

Gallup conducted a study of over 2.5 million teams, measuring 27 million employees for the *State of the American Manager* report, and found the top two reasons people become a manager are 1) being successful in a past role, or 2) having been in a role for a long time.[7]

Neither reason involves the person demonstrating they'd be a good manager or even wanting to be one.

If you've ever been put into a managerial position or asked to lead a team for one of these two reasons, you're clearly not alone.

Others of us *want* to be managers. We love working with people, we want to develop them in their careers, we like coaching, and we enjoy mentoring. Then, we find out the job includes a whole lot of other things—like giving hard feedback, or convincing someone that the job they're not feeling inspired by is something they *totally* signed up for and committed to doing—and we realize managing kind of sucks.

What if we thought about what it really means to us be a manager?

Chapter 2

Great managers, as opposed to bad or mediocre ones, have a strong intention about how they want to show up as leaders. This intention gives them a North Star for communicating with their teams, inspiring people to be their best, and managing the emotions, doubts, frustrations, and fears that naturally come up in the job.

Where We Get Stuck

I'll probably say this every four pages, so get used to it: managing people is hard.

Don't get me wrong—I love people. But let's face it: people are hard to deal with. When we are responsible for helping them reach their career potential and they are *relying* on us for that help, dealing with them gets even harder.

The job of managing is different than most of us imagined it would be earlier in our careers. It's tempting to oversimplify what management involves. Maybe you imagined standing in front of a group of people who were all listening intently to each word you said—or collaborating around a whiteboard, with everyone giving each other high fives while you smiled approvingly at all the amazing ideas being surfaced.

We tend to think, *If I'm good with people, I'll be good at managing.*

My aunt, who is a screenwriter and screenwriting teacher at the University of Southern California, says the same of her students. They think, *Hey, I watch a ton of movies; I'll be a great screenwriter.* Nope, totally different. Just as Aunt Bonnie has to teach her students semester after semester that there is actually a *skill* to screenwriting that they have to learn to get good at it, I'm here to teach you that there's a skill to managing people as well.

Whether or not we wanted to be managers, we often enter the role without a lot of thought. The lessons that we could have gotten a head start on navigating are, instead, learned on our teams.

We think since we're in charge, people will listen to us or at least give us *some* respect. *Spoiler*: In many work environments, simply holding the title of "person in charge" doesn't mean squat. Frustrated when we see no one is really listening, we might shift into overasserting our authority, resulting in turning people off even more. Our teams think we're on a power trip and are even less inclined to do what we ask of them. Great.

We think we'll figure it out as we go, determining what to do next *after* every turn. And we *do* one day figure it out. Of course we eventually do—but at whose expense, and after how long? While yes, most of this will be figured out eventually, it can take *years* to get right.

Think about it: Would you want the person responsible for helping you reach *your* career goals to wing it, hoping they'd pick up some scraps along the way that they could toss to you? Would you want to have a limited understanding of your performance because your manager didn't realize they needed to give feedback? Would you want them to micromanage you because they hadn't yet figured out how to set expectations?

When our team members see that we're winging it or we seem like a fish out of water, they lose confidence in us. They don't trust that

Chapter 2

we're the right person to help advance their career, and in turn, they don't rely on us to support them in their growth because they think there's no point.

A few years ago, I was hired to coach an employee named Nick, who was on a sales team in a startup. Nick was one of the top performers but had a really negative attitude toward his manager, causing major issues between them. When we got on our first coaching call, I asked him to share a little about his frustrations so I could get a sense of where the disconnect was happening.

Nick was outraged about his situation and was eager to share all of his gripes with me. He'd been crushing his sales goals, when out of nowhere, a new manager who had no prior sales experience was hired to lead the team. When she joined the team, she told the group that she'd be learning from them as much as they'd be learning from her, and she said she would just be soaking things up for a while as she got the lay of the land.

Nick felt like this dynamic would lead to a huge step backward in his career. He was hoping for a manager who was a powerhouse at sales and could accelerate him to the next level. Instead, he got someone whom he referred to as "of no use to me."

I've been in Nick's situation, and I can attest to how frustrating it is. You essentially get "layered" with another person between you and the top of the organization. Instead of it benefitting you to have this new manager, you're expected to help that person do *their* job.

But this example isn't about Nick and his reaction—it's about where the manager went wrong. This manager made the same mistake I think many of us make as new managers: in an effort to build connection and be disarming, we completely undermine our own credibility. As a result, our team members are left scared for their own careers.

While I didn't talk to the manager directly, my guess is she didn't come in with a clear perspective or plan for how she was going to communicate the value she brought to the team, even without the sales experience. How she *could have* reframed this is what we're gonna talk about next.

Try This Instead

Becoming a manager is taking on a *new* job. It's not a shifting of responsibilities or adding a few hours of work here and there. It is something completely different from what we were doing before, and now people are relying on us in a totally new way.

Because there are other people involved, we have to bring more to the table. Instead of deciding to figure it out as you go, *set an intention* for how you want to show up as a leader.

An intention is a plan of action.

Think deeply about what it means to be a good leader.

Does it mean that people like you? Or does it mean you bring out the best in people and help them rise to their full potential?

The latter, right?

Does it mean people listen to you just because you're in charge? Or do they listen because you've built up your communication skills, allowing you to inspire a team around a vision and motivate them even when they face change and uncertainty?

People listen more to leaders who talk about the clear direction they are going in. Confidence breeds confidence.

Quick Exercise

Think of three leaders you admire—whether historical figures, past managers, teachers, or coaches—and consider the qualities that make them great, focusing on the ones that feel authentic to how *you'd* show up.

1. Leader 1:
   a. Qualities that stand out:
   b. What you need to do to embody this:
2. Leader 2:
   a. Qualities that stand out:
   b. What you need to do to embody this:
3. Leader 3:
   a. Qualities that stand out:
   b. What you need to do to embody this:

In *The Culture Code*,[8] Daniel Coyle writes about famous UCLA basketball coach John Wooden, who has often been studied for his excellence in leadership after winning ten championships in twelve years at UCLA.[9] One of the qualities that stood out was how he gave feedback on tiny details in the moment—from how players tied their shoelaces to how they passed the ball—that added up to create an unstoppable team. His specific and clear micro-corrections gave team members immediate feedback on what they needed to improve to be their best.

Example
Leader 1: *John Wooden*
    a. Qualities that stand out: *precision and attention to detail*
    b. What you need to do to embody this: *give feedback regularly and in the moment*

Really think about the qualities that are meaningful to you, as opposed to just coming up with a list of famous people's names. Sure, we all might want the success of Steve Jobs, but is his leadership style something that feels appropriate to your current role as a new manager? Or, maybe your ultimate vision of yourself *is* to be like Steve Jobs, and your intention is to exude the vision and tenacity he brought to his work.

There are no wrong answers here—your inspiration could be a parent, a coach, or someone in your community. The point isn't to pick the coolest or most famous leader but rather to be thoughtful and specific.

You might be reading this thinking that the idea of setting an intention is too woo-woo for you, but setting an intention is about achieving results.

Chapter 2

Why This Works

Identifying the qualities that represent how you want to lead will help guide how you show up when things are going well. But maybe more importantly, these qualities will light the path when things *aren't* going so well.

Imagine one of the leaders you aspire to be like is Michelle Obama, because of her wisdom and patience. It's easy to say you want to bring wisdom and patience to your team when all of your team members are awesome and finishing their work on time, without needing a single reminder. The magic of anchoring to some of these "Michelle Obama qualities" is *maintaining* them even when no one is listening to you, two team members quit unexpectedly, and you're pulling weekly all-nighters because your company has a hiring freeze and no backfills and you have to do individual contributor work while managing.

I'll say it again: an intention is a plan of action. And the best plans aren't things we think about loosely in our minds; they are where we put pen to paper. A study in the *European Journal of Social Psychology* found a whopping 91 percent of people who set an intention to exercise by writing down where they would do it followed through on their commitment. Contrast this with the control group, of which only 38 percent followed through.[10]

What is your plan to show up with wisdom and patience when things get hard? Will you start a morning meditation routine to center yourself and get into the present before showing up at work? Will you carve out time every day to do research about your industry and the competitive landscape so that you can be a dot connector on your team? These actions are the plan that follows from setting a clear intention.

When we enter a new situation, we often think about the behaviors we want to avoid. It's almost like self-protection. With managing we might think:

- *I don't want to micromanage.*
- *I don't want to be in the weeds.*
- *I don't want to yell at people.*
- *I don't want to be perceived as cold or uncaring.*

These examples might come to us easily because we've experienced them from managers and don't want to show up this way for our teams.

But what we're often less specific about is what we *do* want to do. Sure, we know we want to be good managers, but what that actually means is different for each and every one of us.

Write the qualities down, identify the necessary actions to embody them, and reread the list regularly. You'll start to build the habit of embodying these qualities.

Imagine company priorities shift, and the project your whole team is working on gets canceled. Not only are you bummed because you've invested a lot of energy into it, you're also worried everyone on the team will want to quit because they feel like their work is being thrown away. Before you react, however, you consider the intention you set. For example: *I show up to challenges with optimism and compassion.*

Instead of getting caught up in a victim spiral or complaining with your teams, you show compassion for their frustration about feeling like their work is being thrown away, while sharing your optimism regarding how the team can still repurpose a lot of the work in future projects. Then, you build a clear plan for how to leverage this work.

In the leadership coaching world, this kind of proactive reflection is called "self-management." It involves being in tune with our emotions and reactions, as opposed to operating on autopilot. This helps us stay grounded and present, rather than getting swept into the drama surrounding a tough situation and regretting how we showed up.

Understand what kinds of things frustrate you or excite you, what kinds of emotions come up when you feel stressed, and what feedback from your own manager you need to actively work on. As a first-time manager, you'll find that so many of the challenges are new, with different triggers showing up every day. There will be personalities you don't vibe with and team members you don't like that much personally. Your job isn't to be everyone's friend; it's to bring out the best in everyone. You'll be positioned to approach that job in a way that is authentic to you when you set an intention and stay consistent with it.

Managing Is a BIG Job

One of the challenges I see new managers face all the time is discovering the job is a lot bigger than they realized, or bigger than the way it was sold to them when they agreed to take it on.

I see you.

We're still doing a ton of the work we were doing before as individual contributors.

Getting people to listen to us is a lot harder than it looks; I mean, *we* did what our managers asked of us right away.

And *waaay* more is out of our control than we realized.

This feeling of lacking control only gets worse when our team members come to us asking us to fix stuff for them that we're not responsible for, and it can cause us to lose sight of our intention and confidence that we can handle the job.

I think this is where we get into the situation that Kate got stuck in at the beginning of this chapter: trying to control how people respond to us instead of how we're showing up.

When it comes to that lack of control, one of the most effective tools I've found to help shift mindsets is from Stephen Covey's book *The 7 Habits of Highly Effective People*. Covey talks about sorting your thoughts into three categories: things you can control, influence, or accept.[11]

I've done an exercise in a number of my workshops for managers, asking them to take a step back and categorize the things they are worrying about. I encourage you to take a few moments to do the same thing right now.

Quick Exercise

Grab a sheet of paper and draw a line down the center. On the top of the left-hand side, write "Control," and on the top of the right-hand side, write "Influence."

Now, think about an area where you've been feeling this "lack of control" the strongest, and start categorizing everything into the two lists. Notice I didn't include a column for the things that are in the "Accept" zone, because frankly, that's most stuff out there. We can't choose who is on our team if we've inherited a team or are reorged into another department. We often can't control budget or when we can hire new team members. We often can't control overarching company priorities.

But there is a lot more in our control than we might have considered before doing this exercise.

As you list what is in your control, think back to the intention you set for how you want to show up as a manager. You have control over your attitude, your mindset, your tone, what you communicate with your teams, your reactivity, and your boundaries. There are even more things on the list that we can influence: hiring for new talent, team priorities, collaborations with other teams, and so on.

All of these things help you show up to work feeling like you are on solid ground, and they set you up to handle the bigger stuff without feeling like things are just *happening to you*.

Example

MY INTENTION: *I show up to challenges with optimism and compassion.*	
Control	**Influence**
Attitude with my team	*Hiring for new talent*
Mindset coming to work each day	*Team's priorities*
Tone of voice and tone in writing	*Collaborations with other teams*

Download a template for this at liagarvin.com/playbook-resources.

Let's return to that example of your team's project getting canceled. Imagine you wake up one morning to an email saying that the project your team has been working on has gotten canceled because of a shift in company priorities, and your team now has a new charter. Your initial reaction might be to think, *This is so unfair! We've been working on this for so long. Everyone is going to quit because all of their hard work will have been for nothing.*

Yes, it is unfair, and it sucks. Let it in, and feel it. Then…let that feeling go.

What you do next will *actually* influence whether or not people quit.

If you think to yourself, *This situation sucks, but I can control how I show up for my team and influence their confidence that everything will be okay,* you might say something like this to your team:

> "I know it was really hard to hear that the project we've all been working on has been canceled, and I can imagine how

frustrated you understandably feel right now. While I'm disappointed by the news too, we are fortunate that so much of the work we've done can be put toward our next project. I will meet with each of you to help you figure out how to leverage your past work for this new direction. I know this also brings up worries about what will happen with your performance review. I will do everything I can to advocate for the work that you did and explain how we're leveraging it to save time on future projects, so the cancellation doesn't count against you."

Such a difference, right?! The canceled project was out of your control, but helping your team see their work will still be valued *is* in your control.

Along with a sense of loss of control can come a sense of loss in general.

Becoming a manager is a change in your position within the company, and it impacts the previous relationships you had. You have a new opportunity in your career, which might be really exciting. At the same time, maybe you were close with a lot of people on your team, and now those friendships have to change shape.

Jaclyn Johnson, founder of Create & Cultivate, shared a story in her business mastermind about one of the biggest wake-up calls that she had stepped into a different dynamic with her team, shifting from friend to CEO. She started her company and grew it with a core set of employees, and she and the team were all really close-knit. But when the company grew to a certain size, the moment she realized everything had changed was when everyone went out to a bar after the company holiday party and didn't invite her. She was the boss; it wasn't cool to hang out with the boss anymore. It felt like a punch in the gut at first, but then she realized it meant they truly saw her as the leader.

Jaclyn was the CEO, so there wasn't really a peer group within her company. In your case, this shift is an opportunity to join a new group of peers: your fellow managers who are going through the exact same things you are.

This is one of the reasons I love leading manager development workshops and programs in companies: not only do people get a chance to grow and strengthen their skills, they also start building a network of peers they can lean on long after the programming ends. I deliberately include time for folks to connect because these new networks are so important. Setting your intention as a manager requires proactively creating the system of support you will need in order to live up to that intention. It's part of the action plan.

What does it look like when we do this work well?

Earlier, I shared the story about Nick, the sales team member who got layered and the mistake his manager made by not bringing her intention forward. I resonated with this guy's story because a similar thing had happened to me years prior, and I had felt the same way: that it was a step backward in my career. I had wanted to be the team's manager, and instead of getting that role, someone else became the manager, introducing a new layer of hierarchy into the mix. Literal lose-lose.

Or at least that's what I thought until I met James, the new manager. Immediately after it was announced that James would lead my team, he reached out to connect 1:1. He shared that he had heard about the great work I was doing and understood why his becoming my manager might be disappointing to me, since it had been suggested that I was next in line for the role. He said his goal was to amplify what I was doing, not create a new layer of approvals, and he committed to helping me get more visibility so that I could achieve the promotion I was working toward even faster.

And he did exactly that.

I hadn't realized I lacked an advocate who was tuned in to my work. My previous manager was much higher in the hierarchy and didn't have day-to-day visibility into my work, which was working against me. By contrast, James opened doors for me, and with his support and advocacy in the next review cycle, I got promoted.

James was one of the best managers I've ever had, and not because he taught me everything I know. It's because he shared his intention to elevate and amplify the work of his teams, and he showed up as he said he would. That's all any of us can do.

Remember, the top two reasons people take on the role of a manager are because they were good at their previous role or they had been in their previous role for a long time—not because they were ready to be a manager or even wanted to be one. Being a manager means your relationship to your work and to your colleagues will change, but that's not a bad thing.

By setting an intention, we take an active role in managing that change, both in finding a North Star and in creating a plan for how to operate day to day. That intention becomes a part of who we are—and there's nothing more important than this consistency to develop trust with our teams.

"SOMETIMES IT IS EASY TO FORGET THAT EACH MEMBER OF YOUR TEAM IS A WHOLE PERSON, WITH ALL THE UPS AND DOWNS AND COMPLEXITIES OF LIFE IMPACTING THEM EVERY DAY. BUILDING TRUST SO THAT YOU CAN GET TO KNOW EACH PERSON AND THE CONTEXT OF THEIR LIVED EXPERIENCE ALLOWS YOU TO SUPPORT THEM THROUGH THEIR LIFE'S JOURNEY. THIS UNDERSTANDING WILL MAKE YOU A BETTER MANAGER AND WILL LIKELY PAY OFF WITH FEWER MISSTEPS ON YOUR PART, AND MORE LOYALTY ON THEIR PART."

—Rachel Smith,
Director at Google

Chapter 3
Establishing Mutual Trust

What's trust got to do with it?
Oh everything? Cool.

When I joined the program management team as a new manager, it was the third manager change they'd had in eighteen months. Needless to say, my new direct reports were skeptical. They had been through the ringer. It felt like every time they got invested in a manager or thought they finally had someone who would invest in *them*, the person would move to a new team, throwing their hopes and dreams out the window.

My first few meetings with the new team members were rough. They didn't believe it when I said I was there to help them achieve their career goals because, well, they had heard it all before. Why would it be any different this time?

I could see just telling them wasn't going to work. I had to *show* them I was different. I had to build trust.

Trust isn't built in one meeting, one week, or even one month—it's something that we build over the longer term, through consistency in how we show up for our teams.

And *without* it, we have literally no hope of having a functioning team, so we'd better get working on it.

Effective and high-functioning teams sit on a foundation of mutual trust: managers trusting team members to do their jobs, team members trusting each other as collaborators, and team members trusting managers to have their best interests at heart.

When any of these areas are missing, you see apathy and stagnant performance. When any of these areas are broken, you see conflict.

Many times, like in the situation I walked into, we become the manager of a team with a trust deficit—a previous manager was toxic, promises were made that weren't kept, there was a revolving door of managers, you name it. When there's a trust deficit, we've got to work even harder to get the dynamic out of the red and into the black.

Where We Get Stuck

Because we're focusing on what's expected of us and want to make an impact right away or are under a lot of pressure as new managers, we often come in hot. We start making demands and laying down the rules as if that's going to do *anything whatsoever* to get people to follow us.

Remember, people don't listen to us simply because we're the boss. Sucks, but true. The ole "because I said so" doesn't work on kids, and it works even less on adults.

But when it comes to the importance of trust, don't just take my word for it. According to a 2017 study by the *Harvard Business*

Review, "Compared with people at low-trust companies, people at high-trust companies report: 74% less stress, 106% more energy at work, 50% higher productivity, 13% fewer sick days, 76% more engagement, 29% more satisfaction with their lives, 40% less burnout."[12]

It can be frustrating when we become the manager of a team and folks don't immediately buy in. We know *we're* going to do our best. We kind of want to say, "Hey, I don't know what happened with your last manager, but I'm not them, so can we just move on?" Even reading that, you know it's not gonna fly.

On teams, trust has to go both ways, but it doesn't mean your team members should have to "prove it to you." This is another place I see new managers get stuck: treating their employees like they're auditioning for a role they *already* have. There are implicit expectations that come with being hired for a role and working at a company in general. We should assume our team members have met that bar and are there to do their jobs well.

As more companies shifted to hybrid and remote work, many managers felt nervous about how they would supervise their team members when they couldn't see everyone every day. I received questions about installing software to track keyboard strokes, eye movement, mouse movement, you name it.

These questions implied that there was no foundation of trust, and being at work in person to double-check progress was the *only way* a manager could confidently know what their team was doing.

Is your team member doing a side hustle while they're at work, making TikTok videos to build their influencer brand each time you don't get a reply to a Slack message within fifteen minutes?

Maybe.

Seeing our team members less often *does* put more of a burden on the manager to have built up trust.

But in the same way putting an AirTag in your thirteen-year-old's backpack isn't going to stop them from hanging out with the wrong friends, installing eye-tracking software or monitoring keyboard strokes isn't going to make them do better work. We have to *trust* people. We have to put in the effort to build it; it's not built through surveillance.

Try This Instead

We build trust by getting to know each other, listening to each other, and reinforcing that predictability in how we show up (based on that good ole intention we set in Chapter 2!).

Brené Brown and Patrick Lencioni, two of the most prolific thinkers and authors on leadership, often talk about the importance of disclosure and slowly revealing things about ourselves so that our teams get to know us and we get to know them.

This exchange could take place in a team meeting, from sharing something fun you did with your family over the weekend to talking about the marathon you're training for and how it's exciting but also totally freaking you out. You don't have to share your deepest, darkest secrets—in fact, you shouldn't—but a glimpse

Chapter 3

into your vulnerable side humanizes you as a manager and opens the door for others to share.

The CEO of LeaderFactor, Timothy Clark, summarized it so well:

> Trust is essentially the predictive understanding of another's behavior. The link between trust and psychological safety is based on my prediction of your behavior based on your pattern of behavior. If I can predict that you won't embarrass, punish, or humiliate me when I'm interacting with you and others in a social setting, I'm much more likely to engage, participate, and release my discretionary efforts.[13]

The more people trust their manager, the more effort they bring; the more we trust our teams, the more control we feel safe letting go of.

It's a two-way street.

We need trust to delegate effectively, to be comfortable putting our team members up for growth opportunities, to be able to give feedback—we need it for literally everything.

Our teams build trust in us through consistency in our actions:

- Was it okay that a team member was late to the daily stand-up the first five times, but on the sixth time you publicly reprimanded them?
  → That inconsistency breaks trust.

- Did you say there was flexibility with a deadline and then get frustrated when the original deadline passed?

→ Again, this breaks trust. If you say something, operate in integrity by honoring it. If it has to change, own it and share any context. Say something like, "Hey, I know I said there was a little flexibility on the deadline, but I just heard back from our stakeholder that they're under a lot of pressure to see the work faster, so it looks like we will have to hit the original dates. What can I do to help you get back on track?"

Simple as that, and you can change course without breaking trust.

We build trust in our teams through seeing consistency in their results:

- Look for opportunities for your team members to stretch and grow, and put them in those situations, potentially finding lower-stakes situations for them to build comfort, like running a team meeting.
- Build up to higher-stakes opportunities like presenting work to executives or high-stakes clients as they get a few successes under their belt and demonstrate they can take more on.

Again, we aren't auditioning them for the job; we're letting them build comfort and confidence before adding more responsibilities to their plate.

The consistency and predictability that we exhibit to our team members establish psychological safety. Amy Edmondson, the pioneer of the concept of psychological safety, describes this as feeling "confident that candor and vulnerability are welcome in their workplace. They believe that they will not be punished or humiliated for speaking up with ideas, questions, concerns, or mistakes."[14]

When we feel safe to make mistakes, we take more risks, get more creative, share out-of-the-box ideas, and think bigger—because we know if we get it wrong, it won't be held against us.

It's no surprise why psychological safety is considered *the* leading indicator of high-performing teams. The safer we feel, the better the results we deliver. Google proved this to be the case in a 2015 study of 180 teams to learn the qualities of the teams that were delivering the best results.[15] Looking across dimensions from co-location to tenure to technical expertise, the results surprised everyone.

Having world-class engineers on your team was great and all, but *nothing* stood out more than having a high degree of psychological safety, which included high levels of taking turns and sharing airtime across the team when people were speaking.

A lot of people have heard about psychological safety but don't quite know how to put it into practice. It can feel a little abstract until you dive deeper, which is why we will dive deeper!

Looking back at Edmondson's definition, she doesn't say, "It's a team where everyone likes each other and agrees with what everyone says." People might like each other when there is high psychological safety because they *enjoy* the feeling of being able to speak up and share, but high psychological safety is not present when people are afraid to rock the boat.

Teams where a lot of people are friends might actually have *lower* psychological safety, because people are afraid that if they disagree, they will be excluded from the in-group. This dynamic is something to keep a close eye on. Comfort in being candid and speaking up is a cornerstone. This doesn't mean it's a free-for-all and people are disrespectful; the assumption is everyone is still respectful as they communicate.

There are horror stories about what happens when you don't have psychological safety on teams, including amputees getting the wrong leg cut off because a nurse didn't feel safe to call out the impending mistake to the attending surgeon, or because the surgeon failed to listen to the nurse when they *did* call it out because they broke rank.

In office settings, a lack of psychological safety often shows up as one of the following:

- Saying "yes" to a workload that you know cannot be accomplished in the stated time frame because it's not acceptable to say "no".
- Noticing an issue that impacts the quality of a product or service but feeling like you're "too junior" to speak up
- People accusing you of not being a team player when you disagree.
- Management or colleagues claiming you are always complaining when you raise a concern.
- People continually agreeing to the suggestions of the most senior person in the room, even though the suggestions aren't feasible to implement.

So, drumroll please...here are things we can do to continually build and reinforce psychological safety.

Tools

Postmortem/Retrospective

A postmortem or retrospective is a meeting where you talk about learnings from a project after it ends, allowing your team to reflect on what went well, what didn't go so well, and what everyone will do differently next time. This debrief fosters psychological safety because it invites everyone who worked on a project to share their thoughts, regardless of their role in the project. The goal of the meeting is to share lessons learned, not to debate issues. It reinforces open communication by focusing on the lessons rather than who is right or wrong. To facilitate these meetings, hold a roundtable discussion where each team member shares three times, in the first round sharing what went well, in the second what could have gone better, and in the third what they will do differently next time. Remind people that the third round is about taking personal accountability, not pointing fingers at something someone *else* should do differently.

Premortem

Why wait until a project has wrapped up when we can anticipate what might go wrong and proactively make a plan to address it? Kinda seems like the better route. With big initiatives or projects that contain a lot of risk, I highly recommend having a premortem to discuss the risks and have folks sign up to be accountable for mitigating each of them. Similar to postmortems, this practice encourages open communication and also serves as a forum to allow people to share risks and concerns when the stakes are lower and emotions are calmer.

To facilitate these meetings, open the conversation by talking about the objective of the project and any constraints, and invite everyone to share hypotheticals with a "no wrong answers" vibe in the meeting.

<u>Wild Idea Brainstorming</u>
When planning new projects or kicking off a complex piece of work, host a "wild idea brainstorm" where everyone is invited to share big, bold ideas. Again, the open communication, sharing of ideas, and invitation of different perspectives all are great builders of psychological safety. In this meeting, start by discussing the objective of the project, and invite people to share wild and out-there ideas for how to achieve that objective. People often don't share an idea because they worry someone else will shut it down, saying all the reasons it would never work. In this meeting, however, *everything* is on the table. When you run it effectively, you'll often find that some of the "wild ideas" are not only doable but actually the best approaches to take.

Team-building exercises and activities are also really helpful to build trust across your team. In his book *The Advantage,* Patrick Lencioni recommends doing what he calls the "Personal Histories" exercise.[16] In this activity, each team member shares about their upbringing, their family, and any significant or transformational moments in their life. I do a version of this in workshops I facilitate with teams, asking targeted questions to give people a little more structure regarding what to share. See examples of those questions in the exercise below.

Quick Exercise

Schedule a team meeting, and let folks know in advance that the time will be used for sharing and team bonding. This notice prevents people from feeling like they are being put on the spot when the meeting has a different structure than the usual routine.

Ask team members to share the following:

- Something they are proud of that is not related to work.
- A significant moment from their upbringing that played a role in shaping who they are.

Again, the point isn't to make your team members share their deepest secrets; it's to give a little window into who they are as people. I encourage you to share your answers to these prompts first to set the tone around vulnerability (striking a balance between oversharing and staying too surface level).

Example

Proud of: I've worked hard to strike the right balance between work life and home life, and I'm really proud that I've been able to coach my daughter's soccer team and attend all of the games this year. This kind of attention is something I didn't have from my parents growing up, and it was really important to me to give to my child.

Significant moment: When I was in high school, my family went on a volunteer trip with Habitat for Humanity to build houses. It changed my life. Coming from an upper-middle-class family, this experience gave me so much perspective on how much we had in our lives, and it made me stop taking things for granted.

Exercises like these deposit currency in your team's "personal relationship bank," building trust and psychological safety, which goes a long way toward fostering collaboration.

You know what else adds money to that bank? Getting together in person.

I'm a fan of hybrid work arrangements—for many years now, I've primarily worked remotely—yet I am *still* a strong proponent of getting teams together in person on some kind of regular cadence. Even meeting quarterly or semiannually goes a long way to help your team members deepen their relationships, and it helps *you* build relationships with your team members. If you run a team that is distributed across multiple offices, the sooner you travel to meet each of those people, the easier you will find your job. Something clicks into place when you get that face time.

I know we don't all have control over a travel budget, and if you have a location-distributed or fully remote team, it might not be feasible to meet all of your team members in person right away. But keep the seed planted in the back of your mind that it's an important goal to work toward, and advocate for an in-person summit or off-site with the leadership of your department to try to make it happen.

Why This Works

At the height of the pandemic, I joined a new team as a manager of five people whom I had never met before. We were all working remotely, and there wasn't an immediate opportunity to meet in person. On this team, everyone had their own distinct scope of work to oversee and operated pretty autonomously, not requiring a ton of support.

At first, I didn't really click with one team member in particular. We'd have our 1:1 meetings, but she often didn't bring anything to talk about and our conversations would fall flat. (I'll cover what to do when this happens in Chapter 4.)

Then one day as COVID restrictions started to lift, she mentioned she'd be taking a bike ride through my neighborhood and asked if I wanted to meet for coffee. Game-freakin'-changer. We had the most awesome conversation, laughed, shared stories, and talked effortlessly the entire time. From then on, our relationship at work evolved, and our 1:1s were transformed. She'd bring ideas to talk about, we'd workshop problems together, and we'd talk about her vision for her career. The difference between our interactions before and after that coffee was night and day.

I share this because it's easy to underestimate the importance of meeting in person. If we've worked from home for a long time, we've gotten comfortable. Yes, it is easier *not* to make the effort to meet, *not* to brave the commute, and *not* to put on jeans instead of sweatpants.

And I'm not throwing shade at hybrid; having more flexibility in our work schedules is something that benefits everyone, especially folks responsible for caretaking. But when you are primarily connecting virtually, finding touchpoints to connect in person will strengthen the relationships between you and your team members as well as giving them a chance to connect with each other.

If you're sitting here reading this and thinking, *Trust is cool and all, but shouldn't my team members just do their freaking jobs because that's what they're getting paid to do?*

I hear ya. And yeah, they should.

If people are legitimately underperforming after multiple attempts to reset expectations and give feedback, or if they behave in a harmful or toxic way, they aren't a fit for the role. But as I'm sure you've observed in your own work, even when team members are a fit, showing up for work because they *have to* isn't the same as showing up and crushing it.

As managers, we need to motivate people on two dimensions: doing their best work for their own career growth *and* doing what is best for the company. It's our job to connect those two things, and trust is the glue that holds them together.

At a big tech company where I do a lot of workshops and programs with managers, there is a clear rubric regarding how to advance from one level to the next, spelling out the differences in how to approach the work at each rung of the ladder. For example, at a more junior level, employees are focused on execution or implementation and excelling at getting things done. In this same role at the next level, employees elevate their approach to systematize the work and help make it easier for *others* to get things done.

Chapter 3

To get promoted, people are supposed to demonstrate that they are *already* fully operating at that next level. The challenge comes when people are working toward the promotion; they may stop wanting to do some of the responsibilities of their *current job*, worrying that it will work against them in getting to their promotion.

The concern is actually a symptom of a bigger issue: a lack of trust that their manager will help them find the right balance and fully represent the impact of their work in a way that doesn't undermine reaching for that next level.

For example, if you ask someone to be the notetaker in an important series of meetings, you can't later say they didn't do enough higher-level work because the note-taking took too much time. When you hear resistance about doing a tactical or administrative task, *that* is the worry people have. Sure, most of us don't enjoy note-taking or chasing down meeting actions, but the real concern is that doing so might come back to bite us.

Frustrated that their team members resist fulfilling the responsibilities of their current role while working toward a promotion, managers often ask me how to strike the right balance. My response: "It's on *you* to tell them why and how that work won't count against them—and to really back that up when it comes to performance review time." Establishing trust is the secret.

If people believe that they won't get penalized for doing tactical work, they won't fight tooth and nail *every time* something comes up. If they believe it will be fine, they'll step up to the plate and take their turn.

All of this makes your job so much easier.

Trust creates a personal investment in solving a problem, a sense of personal accountability. Trust also creates an openness in teams to hear tough feedback when things don't go well or when they don't quite hit the mark, because they know their manager has their best interest in mind.

In addition, trust opens the door to focus on our own growth as leaders. Sometimes we get so buried in putting out one fire after the next that we forget to stop and invest energy in ourselves. As managers, when we trust our teams, we get out of the weeds, delegate better, and get more time to focus on what we need to do to grow in our own careers.

Striking the Right Balance

Trust isn't about saying "yes" to everything and making all of your team members' dreams come true. That would be awesome, but it's not what we're talking about here. There will be times when your team members want something that you cannot give them: a change in responsibilities, a raise, a promotion, the opportunity to become a manager.

Saying "no" doesn't break trust. Setting expectations that you can't actually commit to does.

I strongly caution managers, especially new ones, against making promises they can't keep—or making any kind of guarantees. We never really know what will happen in the future, and committing to something you can't back up will immediately throw trust out the window.

When your team members are worried about something, it's hard not to tell them everything will be fine. But the consequences of being wrong are detrimental.

When the mass layoffs within the tech industry took place in early 2023, I heard them described as "The Great Betrayal," and it sent chills up my spine.

My hunch is that label was coined not because of the layoffs themselves but rather because so many companies said they would *never* do layoffs. That was the betrayal.

We don't want to overpromise, and we don't want to go silent either. When your team is worried about something and you don't know the answers, don't avoid them. With those layoffs came questions about more layoffs, and I saw a lot of managers canceling team meetings and 1:1s because they couldn't handle fielding questions they didn't feel equipped to answer.

Showing up anyway is part of that Spider-Man power and responsibility we talked about. It's part of the job; you can't hide from it.

Quick Exercise

In a team meeting where you know folks are going to bring up topics you can't talk about or ask questions you don't know the answers to, try this:

- Share what you know and what you don't (to the extent that you are permitted to share).
- Talk about how you are working to get informed.
- Share when you will update your team with more information.

Then come back *when you said you would* with an update, or with how you'll continue to pursue an update if you still don't have answers.

This consistency and integrity in the follow-up will show your team members that you are committed to supporting them and, you guessed it, will fuel trust.

Example

"One of the marketing teams was let go last week due to the recent announcements of focusing on fewer markets for next year. At this time, I haven't heard of any additional layoffs. We are in a moment of change right now, and I won't always be informed of everything coming. But in all of the leadership meetings I am in, I always push for transparency, and I will let you know if I have updates or more information as soon as I hear anything."

When I joined the team that had experienced a revolving door of managers, there was no chance of reaching them if I didn't start with trust. It didn't happen overnight, but within a few months, my team members did see that I was approaching my role differently than their previous managers had. I didn't make promises that I would solve every problem or stay on the team forever. Instead, I told them that while I was there, for however long that might be, I would be committed to helping find every opportunity for them to showcase their work and stretch toward the next level.

Trust builds the foundation of a relationship, and we continue to deepen it by getting to know our team members better. How to do this effectively is what I'll cover next.

"IT COSTS US NOTHING TO CARE."

—Shaun Peet,
NASCAR Pit Crew Coach and Chief Kindness Officer at Trackhouse Racing

Chapter 4
Getting to Know Your Team

Building a results-based relationship

When Coinbase released its mission statement in late 2020, many people were immediately up in arms. It read: "Sustained high performance: As compared to a family, where everyone is included regardless of performance, a championship team makes a concerted effort to raise the bar on talent, including changing out team members when needed."[17]

Part of the outrage, I'm guessing, was because late 2020 was a time when many companies were bending over backward to accommodate their employees. After being turned upside down by the pandemic, they wanted to avoid losing any momentum and frequently used the "we are a family" metaphor.

There was a major "we will take care of you" vibe going on, and Coinbase's stance starkly diverged from other startups' ways of communicating their mission statements to attract talent.

But Coinbase's statement captured how most companies, big and small, were always *actually* operating; the others just weren't saying it outright.

Where We Get Stuck

Wanting to be socially accepted is *literally* evolutionarily programmed into our DNA. Millions of years ago, if you got kicked out of the in-group, you could become a saber-toothed tiger's main course. It actually *was* a matter of life and death.

These days, our fears aren't saber-toothed tigers so much as having no friends, but hey, that still stings pretty hard. We want to be liked. We want to be a part of something. It's only natural that, as managers, we want our team members to like and follow us.

As a result, we fall into the trap of people-pleasing: telling people what we think they want to hear or avoiding giving necessary feedback, because we don't want to rock the boat or are overly buddy-buddy with people so that they'll think we're the cool manager. Then we find we've turned our team members into a group of kindergarteners who stay up until 10 p.m. watching *Bluey*, eating last year's leftover Halloween candy all night because they think they run the house. (This is currently the case in my household, and, well, I don't recommend it.)

Only a few years ago, "we're a family" was something we'd heard at work all the time. While it's not the case in everyone's family, the metaphor implied the company had unconditional love for employees, would support them no matter what, and committed to sticking with them through thick and thin. It also implied that *team members* would return this loyalty to their company, without managers needing to put in much effort.

Hopefully you can *immediately* see why this assumption is a potential problem in the workplace. If people aren't delivering results, if their behavior is toxic or brings down the team, or if they aren't responsive to feedback after numerous attempts, they really shouldn't be on the team.

The family metaphor gives low performers a blank check to do the bare minimum because they know there will be no consequences. Unfortunately, this lack of effort impacts not only their own results (I mean, if they're underperforming, they are probably struggling on the results side) but also the results of the team as a whole. A 2015 paper from Harvard Business School found that avoiding hiring a toxic employee saved over twice the cost of hiring a higher-performing employee.[18]

But it goes beyond that. High performers don't want to be on teams where underperformance is tolerated. As a former high-performing corporate employee myself, the metaphor for a family was extremely unappealing. I wanted to be recognized and rewarded for my hard work and the impact I landed. I didn't want to have to carry the weight of my team because other people weren't doing their jobs or, more importantly, because our manager wasn't doing anything about it.

The family metaphor incentivizes the wrong behaviors. And that's the case for managers as well. Remember the stat I opened the book with that around 50 percent of people have left a job because of a bad manager? We need to be held to a standard as well.

The friend one is equally problematic. When you are in a group of friends, keeping the peace is often the highest priority. You don't want to rock the boat, so you don't say things that might need to be said. Why? Because in a friend group, everyone is supposed to be equals. Again, as a manager, you see the issue here, right? It's approaching the relationship wrong. You are not equals; you are higher in the food chain than your direct reports.

When we're stuck in the "wanting to be friends" trap (synonymous with "wanting to be liked"), we avoid giving hard feedback, we set zero boundaries with our own time and energy, and we pick up the slack when work isn't getting done, leading us to feeling burned out.

We also overlook the importance of getting to know our team members on a deeper level—their job-related strengths, weaknesses, goals, passions—because we're relying on the belief that if they like us enough, they will do what we ask of them.

Finally, when things do come to a head, we overreact or get disproportionately upset about something because it's been bubbling under the surface and finally reaches a boiling point. In *Unreasonable Hospitality,* author Will Guidara shares a story about one of his early days as a manager at a high-end restaurant in New York City, when he had a team member who kept coming to work with a wrinkled shirt.[19] He let it go the first time, and the next, and the next. Then one day, he finally flipped out on the team member for disrespecting him by always wearing a wrinkled shirt. The team member was caught off guard—of course he was, because he'd never received any feedback about the shirt being a problem. In wanting to be liked and be cool with the team, Guidara explains, something that would have been a quick fix early on (e.g., asking the team member to run upstairs and iron his shirt the first time) ended up turning into a bigger issue.

Try This Instead

As a manager, you need to manage performance, give feedback, have hard conversations, and make tough calls. It's uncomfortable at times, but your job is to ensure your team delivers results. Avoiding the tough parts doesn't make them any less a part of the job; it makes them even harder when the issue you've been ignoring finally blows up.

Instead of trying to fit into that "friends or family" mold, only to find toxicity has taken over your team *like* mold (see what I did there?), a better definition for your team is that it's a *results-based* relationship, similar to a sports team.

On a sports team, the players are very aware that they must perform well in order to keep their jobs and play in the game. Even if it's a disappointment at the time, they know in the back of their minds that they could be traded or benched at a moment's notice.

My friend Charlie Ruiz, speaker and former professional baseball player in the Colorado Rockies organization, described his experience to me like this:

> To be able to show up and execute every single day, it's an understanding across every single position, every single player, every single person on the staff: you either show up and execute or you don't, and you only get so many chances

to be able to do that, to perform. The reality is someone's coming behind you no matter what, even if you're the top dog. The reality is someone is always coming for your jersey.

This awareness keeps players at the top of their game, fighting to continue wearing that jersey for as long as they can. Unfortunately, somewhere along the line in the corporate world, the excitement of joining a company starts to wear off, and a lot of people come in only to collect a paycheck.

Maybe trading our team members isn't in the cards, but reorgs certainly are. Shifting priorities from the top often result in a need for a different team composition. That shift can mean new projects, canceled projects, new managers, and even layoffs.

It's not personal, it's business.

So why the hell would we keep telling everyone we're a family? I mean we *just* covered how important it is to establish trust.

As a manager, your relationship with your team members is based on results. The family metaphor absolves people of a sense of personal accountability, whereas emulating a results-based sports team reinforces it. You are not a family, and you are not friends. That doesn't mean you are cold and don't care about people, but it's not unconditional either. There are consequences if people don't deliver results, and that's to be expected. Like any professional relationship, success in this one requires us to invest the time to get to know people and their goals, set and maintain boundaries, and hold them to a standard.

How do we set the right expectations around results? We meet with team members, ask them questions, listen to them, and use what we learn to help them achieve the best results they can in their current jobs and careers as a whole.

There are three major opportunities for meeting our team members individually, and some of these meeting types happen more frequently than others: routine 1:1 meetings, career conversations, and performance reviews. We'll dive into each, and I'll share a few strategies for facilitating these effectively so that you get the most out of your time together.

1:1s

I was leading a workshop for product managers within a large tech company when a senior manager asked, "If I'm in project meetings with my team members all week, do I also need to have regular 1:1s with them? I feel like I'm seeing them all the time."

My answer was, and still is, "Yes."

Even if you spend thirty hours a week with that person in overlapping meetings, the answer is still "yes."

Why? In team or project meetings, we're only experiencing what our team members are presenting *externally*: how they talk about their work, interact with others, operate in a group, and so on, all of which is important to observe firsthand.

We don't see what's going on with them *internally*: who they are as people, what they're excited about in their lives, what gives them a sense of purpose in their work, what their goals are over the longer term, and where they're feeling stuck. All of this is what 1:1 meetings will help surface.

But just throwing a weekly meeting on a calendar and calling it a 1:1 doesn't necessarily lead to a productive conversation.

We've all been there. You come to the 1:1 meeting with your team member week after week, and neither of you has much to talk about. Time moves at a glacial pace, and after thirteen solid minutes of small talk and project status updates, you end the meeting early to "give each other the time back." Over time, one of you will send a friendly chat message thirty minutes before each weekly meeting saying, "Anything top of mind to connect on today? I'm good to cancel if you are." And, in no surprise to anyone, you're both good with canceling. The meetings feel unnecessary, you've learned nothing about each other, and you've done nothing to further the relationship.

I want to let you in on a little secret: your team member offering to cancel the meeting isn't a signal that they don't want to have 1:1s in general; it's a signal that they don't find value in *your* 1:1s. Research conducted by Quantum Workplace showed that 63 percent of employees want to have 1:1s at least monthly, with 36 percent wanting them weekly.[20] Our team members want to meet with us; they just want it to be worth their time and ours.

My friend Kerri Jacobs, former Googler and creator of the Leading with Empathy program, sought to learn what behaviors from managers made people feel excluded on their teams (leading them to be less likely to perform their best, innovate, and stay on the team). After surveying over three thousand individual contributors, Kerri found that the two most popular answers were: "cancels meetings at short notice" and "multitasks in my 1:1s."

In my own experience, and based on observing managers around me, managers often see 1:1s as the *first thing* to cancel when they get too busy. I know all too well how slighted I felt when my manager would cancel our 1:1s or be visibly doing other work while we were in our meeting. When I attended Kerri's workshop while at Google, I went on a mission to shout this insight from the rooftops, because it's such an easy issue for managers to remedy.

In Kerri's words:

> For your direct report, their regularly scheduled 1:1 call or meeting with you is arguably the most important meeting of their week. As their manager, you have a disproportionately large impact on their ability to be successful at their job. You act as their coach, you help remove roadblocks, you brainstorm with them, you guide their career development, and more. That time when they have your undivided attention is precious.

So here's the right way to do 1:1s (instead of that other way that I may or may not have done them in the past).

Tool

Make your 1:1s mutually beneficial by taking the following steps:

1. Determine a meeting length and cadence that you can commit to. At many companies I've worked in or with, this is a thirty-minute meeting every week or every other week.
2. Create a shared agenda document that both of you can add topics to. When you share this with your team member, make it clear that you both should be adding stuff, not just you.
3. In the meeting, spend a few minutes building rapport, e.g., asking about their week, their family, and something fun or exciting going on in their work. This shouldn't feel forced. Be authentic and demonstrate genuine interest in them as a person. **Pro tip:** Jot down anything notable so that you can ask about it later (e.g., kid's graduation, softball tournament, etc.) These are life moments you can celebrate with them.
4. During the rest of the meeting, talk about highlights, wins, where the team member is feeling stuck and needs support, approaches for kicking off a new project—things that require more of a conversation.

Note: Keep general status updates to email, your task tracking system, or other forums outside of the 1:1 meeting. If there's a project-related question that your team member wants your guidance on, that's perfect for a 1:1. However, a general rapid-fire rundown of the task list is not the best use of your limited time together, and it will not give you much insight into how your team member is doing or feeling.

Download a copy of my 1:1 template at liagarvin.com/playbook-resources.

Chapter 4

Career Conversations

The next place we get to strengthen this results-based relationship is through career conversations. Career conversations are not performance reviews, and they are not for talking about short-term goals around performance (i.e., within the next six months). These are meetings to discuss your team members' longer-term goals and aspirations, which may or may not be met within their current role or even at the current company. In these meetings, you might learn that they want to open up their own business one day, lead a team, change careers down the line, leave the workforce, become a public speaker, write a book, travel to the moon—you name it.

By learning these goals and people's longer-term visions for themselves, you can start to keep your radar scanning for stretch opportunities within their current roles that will help get them closer to achieving their aspirations.

Pro tip: Knowing these goals is invaluable for delegating. If you can connect something you are delegating to a goal your team member has, they are so much more likely to get on board and take it on than if the task you're delegating feels random.

Back in one of my corporate jobs, managers were required to facilitate two career conversations a year with each of their team members, and I think that is a good cadence, whether you are required to have these conversations or not. A career conversation should look further into the future than the next performance cycle, and I encourage you to keep the conversation at that longer-term time horizon if your team member keeps bringing it back to the upcoming review.

These conversations are for BOTH of you:

- *Your* goal is to understand what your team member actually wants to be doing over the longer term, or at least in the next five years.
- *Their* goal is to communicate their aspirations to someone who potentially has the power to open doors and make things happen.

More of the ownership of the conversation and any follow-ups should sit with your team member since it's *their* career you're talking about, but people don't always know where to start. Help them prepare for this meeting by sharing some questions to think through regarding their goals and interests. (Don't worry, I've shared a template with these questions.)

Your team member should come away with an action plan—or at least a few things they can do to develop skills in an area of interest or get more visibility. Avoid ending the conversation with no action items, because without next steps, what's the point to having the meeting at all?

Between each of the semiannual career conversations, if you notice a team member isn't following up on some of the things you've talked about, let it go. It's on them to be in the driver's seat of their career, and the lack of follow-up is a signal that for whatever reason, this isn't a priority for them right now. If after a few of these conversations, they're never really following up, it's worth revising the goals and asking them if those things are actually important to them.

Tool

Here's a career development conversation outline:

Career goals
1.
2.
3.
Skills to develop to achieve these goals
1.
2.
3.
Training or visibility needed
1.
2.
3.
Committing to action

Action	Due by

Example

Career goals
1. Become a director in the company 2. Write a book 3. Do a TED talk

Skills to develop to achieve these goals
1. Learning how to be a manager 2. Nonfiction writing 3. Public speaking and presentation skills

Visibility needed
1. Build relationships with senior leaders across the company 2. Build personal brand outside of the company

Committing to action

Action	Due by
Take on a summer intern	May
Take a nonfiction writing class	June
Volunteer to give updates at three large team meetings	September, October, November

Download a career conversation template that you can share with your team members to help them best prepare for this meeting at liagarvin.com/playbook-resources.

Performance Reviews

Imagine this scenario: Over the previous six months, your team member has been delivering a mediocre performance. Nothing was a major red flag, but nothing really stood out in a positive way either, and they're definitely not edging closer towards a promotion. Writing the manager evaluation portion of their performance review was a struggle—you had a lot of feedback you wanted to share that would help them improve, but you didn't have any time to check in with them, so you kept it brief and decided to cover some of the bigger issues in the performance review meeting itself. When the meeting starts, your team member shows up bubbly and excited for the conversation. You begin by asking them how they think the last six months have gone. They proceed to list all the work they did, how it was transformational for the business, and how they are so excited for their performance review because this feels like the cycle where they will really be recognized for their great work. You feel like you've been punched in the stomach. *How could they be so out of touch?*

Or what about this: You inherited a team of five people in the middle of the performance review cycle. The previous manager wrote the evaluations, but you are on the hook to deliver the message. Two of the team members were working toward promotions and were relying on this evaluation to be the one to seal the deal. In reading the write-up from the previous manager, it does not look great for these two team members. As the new manager, you have to deliver this message and hope neither person quits. You say, "Hey, don't shoot the messenger—I didn't write these," and abruptly end the meeting. Your team members disagree with everything that's shared and ask to go to HR to have their performance reassessed.

These are two challenging scenarios that happen *all the time.*

The first one is completely avoidable by giving regular feedback and having an ongoing dialogue about where that team member stands in your 1:1 conversations. The contents of a performance review should never come as a surprise. Employees might not *like* the contents or associated outcomes, but everything should be on their radar.

The second scenario is something the manager could handle a lot differently. If you inherited a team right before the performance review conversation, acknowledge the awkwardness of delivering a review you didn't write, and focus the conversation on where to go from here. Is there feedback mentioned that you can help them take action on? Talk about the plan. Is there nothing particularly actionable to hook onto because the previous manager was checked out? Talk about the person's goals and how you can work together to help achieve them from here on out.

> **Tool**
>
> **Performance conversations can be nerve-racking. As much as we want them to go well, we can't control how our team members will respond. Here is a simple process for helping them go smoothly:**
>
> - **Step 0:** *Already* have been giving feedback regularly to your team member so that there are no major surprises in the review.
> - **Step 1:** Share your performance feedback (or any associated performance rating) in advance of the review so that your team member has time to digest it.

Step 2: Talk about the highlights, wins, and accomplishments you want to recognize over the past cycle.

- **Step 3:** Talk about any constructive feedback and development areas you'd like them to work on, with examples of how they can address those things.
- **Step 4:** Ask for any feedback from your team member and how you can continue to best support them in their role.

As managers, it's our responsibility to continually give performance-related feedback. If someone is working toward a promotion, talk about the likelihood of success and plan for getting there. If someone is addressing some performance issues, regularly check in to discuss how it's going and what still needs to improve.

If you realize that you haven't been giving feedback and the content of the review will come as a surprise, acknowledge that in the conversation, setting a plan to move forward instead of going backward.

Why This Works

When doing research for this book, I came across a stat that stopped me in my tracks: 89 percent of managers reported that their team members were thriving; meanwhile, only 24 percent of team members reported they were thriving.[21] Ummmm, what?!

How is there a 65 percent gap in our perception of how our team members are doing?

My guess is the 89 percent of managers who don't have a strong pulse on their teams are the ones skipping out on the 1:1s. Our 1:1s and team meetings give us insight into what is going on in the world of our team members and their projects. They also give us insight into when something isn't working.

It can feel easier in the moment to keep wearing the rose-colored glasses, believing that if no one comes to you with a problem, everything is fine. Yes, that day or week, you spared yourself a hard conversation. But this avoidance only lasts for so long. After a few months, you will face a much harder conversation when a great team member leaves, saying they just don't see opportunities on the team. You might think, *But they never even came to me and asked for anything!*

In a 2023 study, the Gallup organization found that 42 percent of voluntary employee turnover is preventable.[22] *How* do we prevent it, you ask? By proactively talking to our employees.

We meet with them, we listen to what they are saying, we pay attention to their tone and body language, and we watch for shifting enthusiasm levels around their work.

If we notice something feels off, we ask:

- "How are things going for you on the team?"
- "What would make your experience better?"

And if everything seems totally fine, we *still* ask:

- "How are things going for you on the team?"
- "What would make your experience better?"

Employees these days are looking for the best opportunity for themselves. The cost of housing and literally every other expense has been going up. Many employees want a stronger sense of meaning in their work, especially after COVID served as a major wake-up call for folks around how they spend their time at work. As a result, that same Gallup study found employees' commitment to stay at their current companies over the long term was the *lowest* it's been in nine years.[23] Employees might want the company to treat them like they are friends or family, but they won't return the favor. Nor should they, because the company isn't *actually* looking at them that way anyway.

When it comes to all of the change and uncertainty right now, there is very little we can promise to our team members. We can't promise there will be no layoffs, and we can't promise there will be no reorgs (we literally just covered this in the last chapter—*please* don't make these promises).

We *can* promise to do our best to support them in achieving their goals for as long as we're their manager—but only if we know what their goals are in the first place, which is why it's important to have routine touchpoints and conversations.

Building a relationship with our team members helps us plan ahead, figure out where our team is solid, and identify where additional competencies are needed. It helps us recognize and show appreciation for the great work happening (which, as I will cover, is a huge driver of high performance and employee retention). It shows us the kinds of opportunities to keep an eye out for so that our team members have stretch projects and growth opportunities, and it tells our team members that we see them as human beings.

Again, this work is a part of that responsibility we have as managers: it is our responsibility to get to know our team members so that they can deliver on the results in the results-based relationship.

The Power of Caring

Having a results-based relationship doesn't mean we don't care for our teams. In fact, the combination of setting clear expectations, holding people accountable, and demonstrating we genuinely care about them is a recipe for high performance.

On episode 111 of my podcast *Managing Made Simple*, Shaun Peet—NASCAR pit crew coach and chief kindness officer at Trackhouse Racing—talks about the importance of noting key moments in your team members' lives (things you learn in that rapport-building part of your 1:1 meetings and by really listening to them), so you can follow up on them when it really matters.

Shaun shared a story where one of his team members was working late, which didn't make sense to Shaun because he'd noted in his calendar that it was the team member's anniversary. He went outside, found the guy, and told him to go home, reminding him it was his anniversary. As the team member was processing how much trouble he was about to be in with his wife for forgetting their anniversary, Shaun told him not to worry: he'd booked them a dinner reservation, and the team member still had time to make it.

"How do you think he shows up the next day?" Shaun asked me. "All in, right? He's bought all the way in."

That is just a small example of *why* his team members are so committed: they know their managers have their backs.

"It costs us nothing to care," Shaun reminds us. For a NASCAR pit crew, shaving milliseconds off the time it takes to complete a pit stop is the top priority. Caring about the team doesn't mean they don't work to get better and better, fine-tuning their performance every single day. But Shaun knows that the *way* the team gets better is by creating a culture of psychological safety, trust, respect, and care. His team functions more like a sports team than a family, and that's why it works.

The little things matter. During the early months of COVID, knowing that everyone could really use a pick-me-up, my manager Rachel started regularly shipping each member of our team boxes of cookies or treats from fancy bakeries. She paid for these out of her own pocket, because she cared about us and wanted to brighten our days.

While everyone loves to receive a treat in the mail, even something as simple as sending an email out of the blue to ask how a kid's soccer tournament went, say thank you for putting in extra work that week, or encourage people to dip out early on Friday shows our teams we care. But we won't know *how* to show our team members we care if we haven't bothered to get to know them.

Our objective isn't to feel like a family or a group of friends—it's to have strong relationships based on trust, mutual respect, and the delivery of results in both directions. When we have those pieces in place, everyone wins.

With a solid understanding of our team members and a platform of trust, now we can get down to the brass tacks of doing the work.

"SETTING EXPECTATIONS ISN'T JUST ADDING ANOTHER TO-DO TO THE LIST; IT IS BUILDING A PERSONAL INVESTMENT IN THE WORK. THE REASON OR GOAL OF YOUR REQUEST MIGHT BE OBVIOUS TO YOU, BUT IT'S NOT TO OTHERS. WHEN YOU LEAD YOUR REQUESTS WITH THE 'WHY' AND NOT THE ACTION, IT ALIGNS EVERYONE TO THAT REASONING, WHICH IN TURN GETS EVERYONE WORKING TOWARDS THE SAME GOAL."

—Alison Curtis,
Head of Client Services, Skona

Chapter 5
Bringing Out the Best in Our Teams

Setting expectations, giving useful feedback, and making accountability not scary

I knew my manager was a little hands-on, but it was the things he was double-checking that got to me.

"Did you send the notes after the meeting?" *YES.*

"Did you make sure there were enough chairs in the room for the team summit?" *YES.*

"Did you remind people they have to finish their prework twenty-four hours before the meeting?" *YES.*

Of course I did those things. And of course he *knew* I did those things because I *always* did them.

I also brushed my teeth, got dressed, and made it to work on time—all without reminders. Imagine that!

My manager at the time was a prototypical micromanager. No matter how many times I proved myself to be on top of things, the moment he got stressed or felt like he was under pressure, he started to grasp for control and "check in" a little more frequently. And by a little more, I mean *constantly*, about all the things.

But the checking in wasn't the worst part. Seeing that my manager was underwater, I'd routinely reach out and ask to take on more responsibilities. He would say that he was grateful and could use the support, but then he'd never follow up with anything to hand off. He wouldn't let go of control over even the smallest tasks.

Where We Get Stuck

No one wakes up in the morning and says, "You know what? I'm going to check up on the little odds and ends that my team is working on just to bother them and make them spin their wheels."

Of course not.

And yet…the moment the heat rises just a little bit, we're like a moth to the flame.

Micromanaging gives us a sense of control: It gives us permission to check in on every little detail simply because it crossed our minds. It tells us we're helping our team members by ensuring they don't miss a thing.

See how many times I wrote "us" in that last sentence? Micromanaging is about *us* as managers; it's not about our teams. It's a fear of releasing control or discomfort with having any unknowns.

Chapter 5

If you can't quite decide whether you're micromanaging, here are three tells, summarized in more detail in episode 147 of my podcast *Managing Made Simple*:

1. You are in *every single meeting*. If you are in all the meetings your team members have, it's a sign you're holding on a little too tight and aren't giving them the chance to step up.
2. You make *every decision*, either because people think you want to make all the decisions or they don't feel empowered enough to make decisions.
3. People are asking for *more work*. This was the case in the dynamic with my manager above. I could see clearly that he was buried, and he was attending all the meetings. However, when I'd offer to help or ask to take on more work, he couldn't think of anything.

What's the problem with micromanaging? I mean, where do I begin?

First, it signals to our team members that we don't trust them, even if they've been doing a good job. If we did trust them, we'd give them a little space or not keep double-checking everything, right?

Next, it frustrates the team because it's suffocating and makes them feel like they are under a microscope. It's flat out annoying to have to answer a boss's constant questions when you are just getting started on something. Like, give me a minute, please?!

From there, team members stop thinking of creative ideas, because they know they'll just be told to do it our way. What's the point?

But wait, there's more.

They stop trying to solve problems or work through issues proactively because they know we'll just come in and change everything anyway. And they stop raising their hands to take on more work because they know we'll just shut them down.

Micromanagement is an accountability killer.

In order to stop micromanaging, we have to figure out where the fear and discomfort come from. The reason *why* these feelings come up for you will give you insight into how to resolve the issue.

Maybe you worry about your own relevance. This is something I've heard from a lot of managers in my workshops and have experienced myself, wondering, *If I fully let go of some of these responsibilities or am not present in certain meetings, what is my role on the team? Will people wonder what I even do here?* This worry is most linked to the impostor feelings that surface for many of us in a new situation.

Maybe you're concerned that your team can't really deliver the results you need them to. Obviously, this is linked to trust—it could be that sufficient time hasn't passed to feel confident that your team will deliver, or you haven't spent enough time building that trust so that you can let go.

Maybe it's that you're not great at planning ahead and aren't sure what needs to happen in a project until it's underway. Once a team member gets started on a project, you realize you want things to be done in a totally different way. This pattern is linked to a lack of skill around delegating.

Each of these triggers for micromanaging show up for different reasons, but again, they aren't a result of the *team* not delivering; they're about *us* and our relationship with the work.

Okay, fine—what if your team keeps messing something up, and things *only* go right when you're involved in every little detail?

Preventing that, my friends, comes down to building the skills we'll talk about next.

And *spoiler*: Micromanaging *still* isn't the solution.

Try This Instead

Resolving *alllll* of this stuff around micromanaging comes down to setting expectations, giving feedback, recognizing wins, and holding people accountable—conveniently, the skills I'm about to dive into.

Setting Expectations

Expectations are all the little things that need to happen in a project or job to complete it successfully. As managers, we need to set clear expectations around how to approach a project, when we'll check in to review or give feedback, and what success looks like. It's also helpful to have team-level expectations around how we'll communicate (e.g., when to use email, Slack, text messages, or meetings), how to escalate issues, and anything that would help avoid issues by knowing or doing something sooner rather than later.

When I talk about clear expectations, I often get the question, "Isn't that kind of like micromanaging, to set all of those parameters around everything?"

Micromanaging isn't about *what*, it's about *when*.

When we establish clear expectations up front, *before* a person has started working on something, it helps them understand everything they need to know in order to complete that work effectively. When we *don't* establish these parameters up front—instead checking in constantly to make little tweaks, changes, and nitpicks regarding how the work is being completed—we are micromanaging. It's a timing thing.

To get ahead of this problem, we have to think about what our expectations even are for a project or role.

Tool

Consider asking yourself the following questions, as establishing these expectations will set the team up for success:

- What needs to get done?
- What are the specifics around how to approach the work?
- When will you check in on progress, offer feedback, or make approvals?
- What do you expect them to have prepared for these reviews?
- What does "done" look like?
- What does a great job look like?

As the work continues, be ready to clarify expectations as needed at any point or fine-tune based on the needs of the project.

Isn't "clarifying" the same as nitpicking once a project has gotten started?

Why, thank you for asking.

It *is* if you are changing things arbitrarily or based on your own discomfort with not being involved in every detail. It *isn't* if the project starts and there's a step that is unclear, or if someone misses something and you sit down with them to get on the same page.

Tool

The magic of setting expectations all comes down to the framing. If you're resetting expectations mid-project…

Instead of saying:

- "Hey, make sure you do this, this, and this…"

    Try:

- "Hey, I was reflecting on the goals for the project, and I know there's a lot going on, so I wanted to make sure we're all super clear on what success looks like."

BOOM.

When it comes right down to it, isn't every conflict, miscommunication, or general "mis-anything" a product of misaligned expectations? For example:

- We thought someone was going to show up at a certain time, but they kept arriving late.
- We thought the deliverable was what the VP wanted, but they actually wanted something else.
- We thought a particular set of work was enough to get promoted, but it wasn't.

Those are all examples of two parties assuming different sets of expectations.

In a 2024 study of 18,665 US employees, the Gallup organization found that only 47 percent strongly agreed that they were clear on what was expected of them in their jobs.[24] Without clear expectations, how would your team members know what success looks like?

It's a moving target.

The key with expectations is to have a reason and rationale behind them, making it clear that you're not just enforcing your personal preferences because of your work style. That's where my number one tool for setting expectations and getting people aligned around a new process comes in.

Drumroll, please: communicate *what's in it for them*.

Tool

Framing an ask in terms of the **other person's interest** has long been studied as an effective strategy for motivating someone to act. It's used widely in marketing, sales, negotiations, and beyond. Knowing your team members' goals and interests allows you to frame expectations in terms of something they care about.

For example, do you have to fill out a presentation template a certain way that seems arbitrary and annoying? Why, let me explain what's in it for **you**! You might say something like this:

> *"This presentation goes to a really nitpicky executive, and when people don't use the template exactly, the executive focuses on that instead of the content of the presentation. We've been working hard to get you more senior-level visibility and to have these kinds of meetings go smoothly for you. So filling out the template exactly as specified, even if it feels over the top, will help reduce hiccups as much as possible."*

See that? You showed what was in it for that person.

Now, I love devil's advocates (not really), so I know what you might be thinking: What if a team member asks why they have to do something just because an executive wants it done that way?

Well, my friend, because that executive makes the performance advancement decisions and essentially cuts our paychecks. If they're happy with our work, we all win. Cool? Cool.

You probably wouldn't want to say it exactly like that, but you get the idea.

The best part about expectations is they set a clear goal post that your teams can work toward, making it so much easier to give feedback because you have a mutual agreement around what success looks like.

Feedback

Speaking of feedback: it's one of the scariest things for new managers, so if your stomach turns at the mere thought of it, hey, I'm right there with you.

Feedback is information about how another person perceives your actions or behavior. It's neither true nor false and not inherently good or bad; it's just data.

But knowing this fact on the surface doesn't make the idea of giving feedback any easier if we've never learned *how* to deliver it effectively—or if we've tried to give feedback to people and it has always gone poorly.

Who wants to be met with the dreaded, "Oh, you don't like how I presented that project? Well, I don't like how you give feedback."

Let's just get this out of the way right now: there will be plenty of times when you give feedback and it doesn't go well. A lot of people struggle with hearing they need to improve something, even if they tell you they love feedback. In fact, I've found it's usually the people who say they love feedback who are the *worst* at receiving it.

Like people who say, "I hate drama"—oh, you *know* they love drama.

To understand where our team members—and, frankly, all of us—get stuck when it comes to feedback, let's explore some of the triggers. "Feedback trigger" is a concept from Douglas Stone and Sheila Heen's book *Thanks for the Feedback*, which breaks down the three places that most trigger people:[25]

1. Truth—we believe the feedback is fundamentally inaccurate, so we feel wronged by the situation.
2. Identity—the piece of feedback hits on something we were already insecure about, so it cuts to the core of our existing impostor feelings.
3. Relationship—it's not the feedback we have an issue with but who said it; like, who is *this* person to come to me with that?

When I worked in tech, I had a lot of impostor feelings about not having an engineering background, and I worked hard to become versed in the technical details of the work I was involved in. In one of my roles, we had to solicit peer feedback for our performance reviews, and it felt like a knife through the heart when a random team member whom I barely worked with wrote something along the lines of "Lia would benefit from becoming more technical." Reading this, ALL THREE TRIGGERS fired at once.

First off, not true—I totally understood the technical details of the work, thank you very much, and could even go head to head with engineers to debate them. Second, there we go again feeling not good enough for not being an engineer. And third, who the hell was this person to come up with this feedback when we *barely* even worked together?!

> **Tool**
>
> As managers, when delivering feedback, we need to be conscious of these triggers so that we can make sure to step around them:
>
> - To avoid hitting the **truth** trigger, make sure you're being specific and bringing concrete examples instead of talking in generalizations.
> - To avoid the **identity** trigger, talk about what is going well along with what needs to improve, recognizing when this piece of feedback could touch on a sensitive area. The goal here is to contextualize the *one* instance so that the person doesn't spiral.
> - To avoid the **relationship** trigger, do all the up-front work that I talked about in Chapters 3 and 4, so your team members are crystal clear that your feedback has their best interests in mind.

Our job as managers isn't to deliver feedback as if we're a UPS driver dropping off a package—*here you go, do with the message what you will.* Our job is to deliver it effectively, in a way that supports our team in internalizing the content.

One helpful lens to share with your teams is to think about receiving feedback through a strainer rather than a sponge, as discussed in the TEDx Talk "Why You Should Use a Strainer Instead of a Sponge to Process Feedback."[26] The talk suggests that you listen to feedback with curiosity—without getting too thrashed by believing you have to implement everything, or so avoidant that you don't need to take anything to heart.

If you have team members whose strainer holes are a little too wide and shrug everything off, connect the feedback back to their career and performance goals, asking them to consider what value they can glean from it, even if they don't fully agree. Alternatively, if you have team members who hold on to every bit of feedback like a sponge, encourage them to collect more data points to get a wider perspective on how they are perceived.

The biggest reason why feedback is scary is we often equate it with being only the bad stuff, or the things we have to change about ourselves. We've got to demystify this for our team: as data, feedback can be positive just as often as it is negative.

Here's a quick hack to reframe the bias that feedback is always negative: start saying to your team members, "I have some great feedback to share with you" or "The VP was so excited about your work. Here was their feedback."

By pairing "feedback" with positives, together we can rebrand this whole "feedback is bad" misconception.

The other hack is to lean on the expectations you set. Yeah, that was one of the main reasons for setting them in the first place.

Feedback is easy to dismiss or discount when it doesn't feel like it's based on anything. Pair an insight with an expectation, and it's harder to discount: "This was the expectation we talked about, and unfortunately, it wasn't met."

The same goes for positive feedback. It feels kind of meaningless if there wasn't any particular expectation. But if you connect the feedback to how someone knocked it out of the park, now they're flying high: "This was the expectation we talked about, and here is what you did to crush it!"

When we anchor feedback to expectations, everyone is on the same page.

How can we give effective feedback? My favorite feedback framework of all time is Situation-Behavior-Impact (SBI), created by the Center for Creative Leadership.[27] If you're a follower of my work, you know I *always* talk about this framework, and I'm not sorry about it. I'm also known to throw on Miley Cyrus's "Party in the USA" from time to time because, as with SBI, it's THAT FREAKIN' GOOD.

> **Tool**
>
> The SBI framework helps you share a piece of feedback with clarity and specificity. This feedback can be either positive or constructive. (In fact, it works really well for reinforcing positive behaviors you want to see more of.) Frame the feedback in terms of the following:
>
> - Situation: Specifically, where/when did this thing take place?
> - Behavior: What was the behavior (i.e., what happened)?
> - Impact: What was a result of that behavior, positive or negative, based on the expectation?

I love to pair this kind of feedback with a request, saying, "Based on this, next time will you please…" and asking something specific so that the person on the receiving end understands how to take action.

Example

"In the team meeting this morning that you were facilitating [situation], when the conversation started to go off the rails, you stayed calm and, with your thoughtful questions, got the group back to a productive conversation [behavior]. With such a tight project timeline, it's so important to utilize these meetings to make decisions, and because of your awesome facilitation, we were able to come to a decision everyone was aligned with [impact, reiterating the expectation]. I know it might have felt a little uncomfortable in the moment, but that was great leadership, and I'd love to keep seeing more of that in future meetings [the request]."

Grab my Feedback Mad Libs cheat sheet to help streamline your next feedback conversation at liagarvin.com/playbook-resources.

When having a harder conversation or delivering news that I know a team member won't be excited about, I layer in a few more strategies that I'll walk through next.

The Power of Taking Responsibility

In one of my roles in big tech, I was both managing a team and helping managers in our department with their team strategies. Right before performance reviews, one of the managers came to me completely torn up. He had a team member who was going for a promotion that review cycle and was pretty confident it would happen—and this manager had even told the team member it was in the bag. Unfortunately, on the team, promotions were determined by a committee, and the rest of the group didn't agree it was quite time for this employee. They denied the promotion, and the manager had to go back to his team member and deliver the news. He felt terrible, and he came to me to talk through how to navigate that conversation.

I told him to bring the same level of compassion and sense of personal responsibility that he was expressing to me to the conversation with the team member. My guess was it would go a really long way for her to see that he recognized his own missteps in the situation. How he handled the conversation was a master class in managing hard moments.

The manager started the conversation by sharing that he had some hard news to deliver and understood it would be really disappointing. He said he would have been devastated as well if he were in her shoes. He told her the promotion didn't happen, apologized for saying that it was a certainty when he didn't have that guarantee, and took responsibility for how it must feel hearing the news. She got upset, and he sat there with her in the meeting, giving her space to feel her emotions without judging them. She said she was going to quit; he said he understood that he had let her down. When the moment felt right, he said he'd learned which factors had blocked the promotion and that he was committed to helping her close those gaps. When she was

Chapter 5

ready, they could regroup to talk about those details and how to proceed.

She agreed, and the meeting ended. He checked in with her the next day, again apologizing and taking responsibility for where he had overpromised. When they met a few days later, he shared that the biggest piece of feedback was that in moving so fast to get her work done, she didn't always bring other people along into the process, which made it seem like she wasn't a strong collaborator. They discussed some ways to do this better.

With support and encouragement, this team member became the *best* collaborator and was a shoo-in for the promotion the following cycle.

Let's recap the skills this manager demonstrated:

- He took personal responsibility, recognizing where he'd gone wrong in the situation and apologizing.
- He held space for emotions, allowing the team member to feel the feels without judgment.
- He talked through the gaps and shared how he'd support her in closing them.

After this situation, the manager and his team member were closer, and both of them knew they could handle difficult situations that felt almost irreparable in the moment.

> **Quick Exercise**
>
> Consider a difficult conversation you have coming up that is making you feel uneasy.
>
> Write out what you can do for the three steps:
>
> 1. Take responsibility.
> 2. Hold space for emotions.
> 3. Offer support to close the gaps.

Recognition and Appreciation

Recognizing the great work happening on your team (big things and small) and showing genuine appreciation are some of the *most* important things you can do for your team members—and are commonly underutilized.

I think some managers don't realize the importance of showing appreciation. They're busy and will recognize a big win when something stands out, but communicating appreciation is not top of mind. Others subscribe to a "no news is good news" philosophy, believing if they haven't said anything, their team members should *assume* everything is going fine. Also, because communication styles vary widely depending on your culture, upbringing, and past work experience, you are likely to have a different communication style from your team members.

Let me let you in on a little secret: the more people feel seen and appreciated, the *better* work they do, and the *easier* your job becomes. So no matter the level of recognition you're giving people today, it's time to turn it up a few notches.

Chapter 5

When it comes to the importance of recognition, there's no shortage of research:

- Employees who feel like their work is *not* recognized are twice as likely to quit their jobs, and employees who feel their work *is* recognized are twelve times more likely to deliver great results.[28]
- Recognition drives results, yet we're not seeing enough of it. In a survey by TalentLMS, 28 percent of workers said they rarely or never received positive feedback from their managers.[29]
- It's not enough to offer appreciation sometimes or when we think of it. A 2013 *Harvard Business Review* article cites research that employees need a six-to-one ratio of positive to constructive feedback in order to stay motivated.[30]

While some of us might feel like we're risking crossing the line into participation awards, this research does not suggest giving someone a gold star just because they bothered to show up to work. Recognition that motivates people has to be *genuine* and *specific*.

A well-written email response, a meeting someone helped keep on track, a lunch setup for a new team member to make them feel welcome—these are all examples of seemingly small things that go a long way toward building a positive culture on your team, and they are great behaviors to recognize.

How can we make recognition genuine and specific? Use the ole SBI framework. It is the literal gift that keeps on giving. Share a situation where someone rocked it, describe what they did, and celebrate the impact it had on the team. The more specific we are, the easier it will be for the person to reproduce that behavior.

But it's not just the act of recognizing work that matters. The *way* in which we recognize it helps ensure that the message really lands. Does your team member like public recognition (e.g., sending an email to the whole team) or private appreciation (e.g., sending an email just to that person)? It can be easy to default to our own personal preferences, thinking that of course our team member would want to be recognized in the same way.

Let's say you love public recognition and being in the spotlight. Thinking everyone loves to be recognized by the full team, when a team member gets promoted, you make a special announcement in your team meeting and ask that person to give a little speech. Unbeknownst to you, being in the spotlight is your team member's *worst nightmare*. Not only do they not feel recognized, they're also frustrated that you put them in that situation. Whoops.

As managers, it's not our job to recognize or appreciate people in the way that *we'd* want; our job is to (when possible) do it in the way *they* want.

> **Tool**
>
> **Ask your team members to share how they like to receive positive and constructive feedback, and honor that request when possible. Create a "feedback cheat sheet" for them, whether in a written log or in your memory. Refer back to it to have a sense of how each of your team members prefer to receive positive or constructive feedback in order for it to land best.**

Example

Feedback Cheat Sheet
Positive Feedback / Recognition

- *I don't love being put on the spot, so I prefer to receive any recognition one-on-one instead of in front of the whole team.*
- *I'm really working to get more visibility in my role, so when something good happens and it feels appropriate, please pass positive feedback or recognition of my work on to our VP.*

Constructive Feedback / Difficult News

- *I like to be sent an email with the hard feedback or news so that I have a little time to process it, and then have a meeting to discuss further.*
- *I like hearing what's going well along with what isn't working so that I have a sense of where I stand on the whole.*

As you have a conversation about this topic, share how you like to receive feedback as well. Feedback has to be a two-way street on your team, and your team member should respect your needs when it comes to feedback, just as you're respecting theirs.

Accountability as Ownership

You know those teams where everything feels *so much harder* than it needs to? Decisions are continually being reopened. Work takes longer than it should. There's constant finger-pointing and blame.

These difficulties all signal an issue around my favorite topic: accountability.

If you've followed any of my work, you know my perspective on accountability: it is the single biggest issue on teams. And if you're new to my work, hear this: accountability is THE SINGLE BIGGEST ISSUE ON TEAMS.

When I talk about accountability, I mean bringing a sense of *ownership* to our work. To illustrate what this means, consider the difference between renting and owning a home. Here's how I explained it in my book *Unstuck*:

> When you rent an apartment and you have a leaky faucet, you call the landlord and they are on the hook for sending someone over to fix it. They might hire the cheapest person possible (or their non-plumber friend who ends up half-assing the job), but they send someone and they pay for the labor. In this scenario, sure, you care about the apartment, you want it to be kept in good condition, but the responsibility to make major repairs lies with the owner, not you.
>
> Owning a home is a whole new ballgame. When the plumbing breaks because you used too much toilet paper (even though your parents taught you better), tough luck. It is 100 percent YOUR problem now. You have to find the repair company, you have to meet them at the house, and, of course, you have to pay them. You also have to sit there as they snake hair out of the shower drain and look at you in disgust after you said "not sure what happened" when they asked how the drain got clogged. If you are too busy to call the plumber, can't

afford their services, or feel like it's someone else's problem to solve, the plumber doesn't come and the issue doesn't get fixed. Because you've committed to ownership of the house, you're responsible for it, whether things are going well or not.

Similarly, owning something at work means being on the hook for it from a time, cost, and responsibility standpoint. Yet when we're faced with owning an outcome, more often than not, in environments striving to be collaborative and give credit to all people involved in solving a problem, we avoid putting one person's name on the line for a task. We shuffle our feet when it's time to step up to the plate and have difficulty taking ownership—likely because we don't want to be left with the career equivalent of an overflowing toilet. But sadly, it's the avoidance of accountability that will leave you alone in the middle of the night with the plunger in hand.[31]

We want our team members to treat their jobs as owners, not renters. When they feel a sense of ownership, they approach their jobs in a completely different way. They bring solutions when they encounter a problem, instead of throwing their hands up and asking us to figure it out for them.

When everyone acts as an owner, there is a shared sense of accountability for committing to the deadlines set, decisions made, and plans established. People don't want to let down the group, so they show up as their best.

Now, our teams won't just feel accountable because we tell them they should. They'll feel accountable when we've set clear expectations, delivered feedback and followed up on it, and recognized their efforts and accomplishments. It's *these* actions that make them want to be owners.

In the same way our teams will more likely meet the expectations we set when they understand what's in it for them, they feel accountable when they understand the *why* behind what we expect them to do. I mean, would you want to "own" something that you didn't fully understand?

Years ago, I was managing a program management team, and documenting projects was one of the major performance expectations for their role. One team member was awesome at their job, motivated their team to finish their work on time, and had great relationships with stakeholders. But when it came to documentation, they fell short.

I brought this up in one of our 1:1s, asking where some of the documentation was for the last few projects. They answered, "Oh, I'm not playing the documentation game."

This caught me off guard. I mean, let's be real: this whole "work thing" is a game to some extent. Whether you like it or not, you've signed up to play the game. But it was a clear indication that somewhere along the line, no one had explained the context for *why* the role required documentation. Based on this person's response, I sensed that telling them they had to do it so that it would look good on their performance review wasn't going to fly.

Instead, I started in with some "why" magic. I told them that the reason documentation was such a key part of the program management role was so that people could see the thinking behind the work, which can often be invisible or underestimated. When we documented where the team got stuck, what approach we took, and the result we achieved, it showcased the transformational impact we had on the work.

In that moment, their whole demeanor changed from "I'm not going to do that" to "Oh, sh*t, I should have been doing that the whole time." With a clear *why,* they got on board right away. They felt accountable.

But the biggest thing about having a sense of ownership isn't just that we take pride in something; it's that we understand the buck stops with us. Our teams stop being accountable to expectations when we don't check back in or follow up. They start reopening decisions, missing deadlines, and dropping balls when they know there is no consequence for not delivering.

Quick Exercise

Make a list of challenge areas on your team where you've seen some lack of accountability showing up. Then, consider what you can do to get the ball back in your team's court. Essentially, what accountability mechanism do you have at your disposal? How will you deploy these and at what frequency?

Challenge area:
Accountability mechanism:
When and how you'll use it:

Challenge area:
Accountability mechanism:
When and how you'll use it:

Challenge area:
Accountability mechanism:
When and how you'll use it:

Example

Challenge area: *Team members aren't hitting their target metrics for the number of customers served and are not taking ownership of what to do about it.*
Accountability mechanism: *Have each team member be responsible for reporting their numbers, instead of me, the manager, communicating the numbers to them for them to comment on.*
When and how you'll use it: *Ask each team member to present their numbers in the weekly meeting, along with a plan for how they will hit their target if they've missed it.*

Download a template for this at liagarvin.com/playbook-resources.

Why This Works

Managing requires us to look at our team's work from a different altitude than we might be used to. The bigger picture, the interdependencies, the load balancing: all of these require us to take a step back and make a plan before we dive into the doing.

Chapter 5

Many new managers struggle with operating at this altitude instead of in the details; they wonder, "How do I add value?" or "Where do I fit into the picture?" The answer lies in *enabling* your team to be as effective as they can be, which requires implementing all of the tools from this chapter.

Set clear expectations with your team members around how to track work, what to share when you check progress, what "done" looks like, the difference between a good job and a great job—all the guidelines that show them what they need to do to be successful.

With expectations set, you now have something to anchor to when you give feedback, so it doesn't feel arbitrary or subjective—people can act on it or take it into consideration. Most of the time when feedback is contentious, it's because someone didn't think it was fair or warranted. Delivering feedback that someone didn't hit the mark is always gonna be tough. It goes *so much better* when you can link it clearly to an expectation you set.

Feedback is the lifeblood of bringing out the best in our teams. If we avoid giving it regularly because we're afraid the conversation might not go well or that someone will be defensive, we're holding that person back from realizing their full potential. It's not fair for us to avoid feedback just because we aren't skilled at it. Let's practice it, get more comfortable with it, and make it a regular thing.

When giving feedback, frame it in a way that will land best for your team member. In a manager training I facilitated once, a participant said he liked hearing tough feedback in a way that was direct and to the point. He felt like he was coddling his team members by sharing things that were working well in those conversations, because that's not the way *he* would want the message delivered to him.

I stopped him and said, "It doesn't matter how *you* would want to hear the feedback, does it? You are giving feedback *to your team member*, not yourself. What you'd want to hear has literally no bearing on the conversation."

Take the perspective of your team member: Is the feedback hitting on one of the triggers we talked about? Are they new to the team and just getting their footing? Do they have a very different communication style from yours? Then curate the message accordingly. Lean on the insight you gleaned from the "feedback profile" conversation.

Feedback isn't just the stuff folks need to fix. By sharing regular recognition, appreciation, and positive feedback, we reinforce the behaviors we want to see more of.

Clear expectations, feedback, and recognition fuel accountability. And following up on all of this keeps the jet engine moving. As team members begin to step up as accountable owners, their relationship to the work changes—as does yours. Their proactive problem-solving frees you up to focus on how to grow the team and be more strategic, because you aren't going in circles around something your team member should figure out. This sense of ownership brings more enjoyment to the work and helps folks take pride in it—and the overall output improves.

Remember, being a manager comes with a lot of power, even if you don't feel all that powerful. Your team is looking to you for guidance, direction, and follow-up; show up for them in the way they expect you to.

With the foundation of expectations, feedback, and recognition driving accountability, our team members are fully equipped to solve problems without us jumping in to fix everything. That is, of course, if we let them.

"LISTEN AND LEARN FIRST. LISTENING IS NOT PASSIVE—WHAT'S THE TEAM SAYING?—BUT TAKING THE TIME TO SPEAK TO INDIVIDUALS ON THE TEAM, MAKING TIME TO LISTEN AND MAKE A HUMAN CONNECTION. ALL TOO OFTEN WHEN WE ARE PUT INTO A POSITION OF POWER WITH MANY CHALLENGES, WE ARE BIASED TO ACT, TO WANT TO "FIX' THINGS. RATHER THAN ACTING FIRST, LISTEN FIRST TO UNDERSTAND WHAT ARE THE REAL ISSUES, WHAT HAS BEEN DONE, WHAT ARE THE CHALLENGES. LISTENING ALSO CREATES EMPATHY; LIKE IN ANY DESIGN PROCESS, YOU NEED TO EMPATHIZE WITH WHAT THE TEAM IS GOING THROUGH. A CHANGE, LIKE HAVING A NEW MANAGER, WILL CREATE ANXIETY AND UNCERTAINTY FOR THE TEAM."

—Albert Shum,
former Corporate Vice President of Design
at Microsoft

Chapter 6
Freeing Up Time to Truly Lead

Unlocking the secrets to delegating, coaching, and not trying to do everything ourselves

I was running a group coaching session with a set of managers to talk about what they needed to feel supported in their roles. These managers were burned out, and everything we talked about kept coming back to one thing: they needed more time.

"I'd love to not have to constantly move my 1:1s…"

"I'd love to have more meaningful career conversations…"

"I'd love to be more mindful of stretch projects and opportunities for my team members…"

"I'd love to take a step back and look at where I'm going in my own career…"

"…but I just don't have any *time*."

Between representing the work happening on their teams in reviews and project meetings, shielding an already over-capacity team from getting more work piled on them, and connecting the dots among projects, they felt at a deficit every single day by the time they went home.

But as I started to peel back the onion a little bit, I saw the problem wasn't time—it was that these managers were missing opportunities to practice two of the most effective time-management skills for leaders: delegating and coaching. As a result, they were involved in *every little thing* that came up on their teams. The solution wasn't to find more hours in the day; it was to refocus the hours they did have on the *right* set of activities.

Where We Get Stuck

When I asked this group of managers how much work they were delegating and how much they were coaching their team members to solve problems on their own, the question baffled them. It seemed impossible to delegate work when they themselves felt so underwater, and they couldn't imagine dumping even more work onto their teams.

But the issue wasn't with the delegating itself; it was the interpretation of delegating being "dumping work onto their teams."

And these weren't the only managers whose faulty definition of delegating was holding them back. In a group of business owners and entrepreneurs I'm a part of, we began the year by committing to accomplishing a stretch goal that we'd report on at our end-of-year meeting. When it came time to share whether we'd hit our goals, I heard at least five business owners say that they'd "cheated" by delegating a part of the task to their teams.

I wanted to jump out of my seat and yell, "DELEGATING ISN'T CHEATING. IT'S *LITERALLY* WHY YOU HAVE PEOPLE ON YOUR TEAM!"

Delegating is the act of reassigning a task or responsibility to another person. In a perfect world, it allows our team members to learn a new skill, stretch themselves into a new area, get more visibility, or take on more leadership opportunities. It allows us as managers to scale our own impact, get out of the weeds, and free up time to focus on other things.

But even with all of these benefits, delegating is one of the places I've seen managers struggle the most.

As a new manager, you might not be a great delegator. You've probably never had to do it before. Delegating effectively requires a mindset shift regarding how to look at a task or project; it's reframing our relationship with a piece of work. Instead of doing the work ourselves, we have to set the conditions that will enable *someone else* to do it. When that task is something we have done a lot before or do intuitively, it can be really hard to articulate how someone else should do it.

But we don't just struggle because it's hard to explain how to do something. When we have trouble delegating, it usually comes back to trust. We either don't totally trust our team to do the thing, or we don't trust ourselves to explain it well enough for someone else to do it right. This doesn't mean we dislike our team members or think they can't do their jobs, but some obstacle prevents us from fully stepping back.

I was running a workshop with a team of engineering managers when someone asked, "If I delegate something to a team member, won't people wonder what I'm even doing here?"

No, dude.

Delegating doesn't mean you hand off your whole job and sit back on a lounge chair sipping mojitos. It means looking across a task or set of work, considering all of the pieces involved, and then identifying parts that someone else could take on. This might be a whole project, a part of a project, a meeting, a report, or something else. It's not all or nothing.

Take, for example, preparing for an executive presentation. Doing that "task" includes collecting all the inputs, designing a slide deck, facilitating a meeting, capturing actions, sending a follow-up—any of those steps could be broken out and done by another team member.

One of the biggest challenges managers share with me is feeling spread too thin across too many meetings. With so many commitments on their calendar, they struggle to find enough time to connect with their team or get their own work done. A 2017 *Harvard Business Review* article states that managers spend about twenty-three hours per week in meetings.[32] For many of the managers I work with, it's more like thirty hours.

If you're in that same "meeting overload" boat, I've got to ask: How many of those meetings also include your team members?

Seventy percent? Eighty percent? When I dig into the issue with managers, I often find the vast majority of their meetings overlap with one or more of their direct reports. Yet when I ask if they also have to be there, the answer is an overwhelming "*Of course* I do."

It's totally fine to be there at the beginning if you're helping to define a strategy or someone is getting up to speed. But as time goes on, really consider: What meetings could you step out of and allow your team members to take more of an active role in?

"But my team members want me to be there!"

Oh, I've heard it all before. And I want my mom to call Comcast for me every time my bill unexpectedly goes up, but she keeps saying "No," and I've managed to take care of it myself.

Sure, your team members might think it's awesome that you attend all the meetings—representing the work of the team, fielding the hard questions, and remembering all the follow-ups. It would be pretty great not to have to deal with that stuff. But by being there, you take away their opportunity to learn how to do those things or build confidence in doing them, and then you can't step out even if you want to.

There's also the possibility that your team members *want* the opportunity to take more of an active role in the meetings but don't step up, because you are there "representing the work of the team, fielding the hard questions, and remembering all the follow-ups." Maybe just a little?

"But there's *soooo* much context they need in order to represent our team well in the meetings!"

Context is important. But there's a degree of important context that's possible to translate, and then there's knowing every single thing under the sun that *you* know, which is way more than what's needed for that one meeting.

Meeting overload is a symptom of an issue; it's not the issue in and of itself. It points to a fear of delegating and an ineffective flow of information on a team. When you focus energy on addressing the information flow, as opposed to having everyone sitting through meetings to make sure they don't miss anything, everyone will get to spend less time in meetings, including yourself. Addressing this difference includes understanding how information flows in and out of project meetings, how decisions are made and where people can weigh in, how decisions and approvals are communicated downstream, and so on.

In the coaching group I mentioned at the start of the chapter, the managers also didn't quite get what I meant by coaching their teams to solve problems on their own.

Another trap we can fall into is thinking we're the right person to handle certain pieces of work on our team—or, in some cases, are the default person to take on a responsibility—simply because we're the manager.

As high-achieving professionals, we are hardwired to solve problems. Someone comes to us with an issue, and we want to fix it, especially if we already know the answer. It's easier and faster that way—why not, *right*?

Wrong.

Solving everything for our team is problematic for multiple reasons. First and foremost, always jumping in is a recipe for spreading ourselves too thin and burning out. The bigger our team grows, the more plates we have to keep spinning, and soon we won't be able to sustain the workload.

But that's not even the biggest problem. The bigger issue is that jumping in with our superhero cape prevents our teams from being accountable for figuring things out themselves, which we literally *just* identified as the most important quality of a team.

No big deal.

When we run in and grab the steering wheel each time someone is about to take a wrong turn, we don't give them the opportunity to *maybe not even make that wrong turn*—or to make that wrong turn but eventually find their way back to the right path.

Try This Instead

Our misunderstanding and avoidance of delegating and coaching are keeping us stuck and preventing our team members from taking on more meaningful responsibility.

Delegating

Let's start by myth-busting delegation once and for all.

Tool

Delegating myth #1: "I don't have time to stop even for a minute to figure out what to delegate."
- **Solution:** Record a voice note or Loom video as you perform a specific task, walking through everything step by step and describing the exactly way you are doing it.

Delegating myth #2: "My team members are already completely overloaded; how can I add something else?"
- **Solution:** Time-box the request (i.e., ask them to work on the task for no more than five hours), or hand off a smaller piece of work that is more manageable.
- **Solution:** Understand what their workload is, and if they are over capacity, balance the load of existing work on their plate to make room for the new thing (if the new thing is more important).

Delegating myth #3: "I tried to delegate something, and my team member refused the request."
- **Solution:** Consider a career goal that a team member has shared that you might be able to connect this work to. Doing so demonstrates what's in it for them and strengthens your relationship by showing that you look for opportunities that will benefit them.
- **Solution:** Time-box the request. This is especially helpful with tactical or administrative work that folks are resistant to taking on. Example framing: "With Joe leaving the team, I'm going to need you to step in and take notes for the executive review for the next three meetings. They are only sixty-minute meetings, and after three, I will hand this off to another team member."

Delegating myth #4: "This project needs so much context; I can't expect my team member to learn everything."

- **Solution:** Write down what context they *absolutely* need, or have someone shadow you one or two times doing the task. The caveat here is not to wait to delegate until the last minute and then get frustrated if they don't know how to do something you've been doing by yourself, just because *you* didn't plan ahead.

Delegating myth #5: "If I delegate everything, how will I fill my time?"

- **Solution:** There's an infinite number of things we can do as managers that do not consist of being in the weeds with all of our team members' work. Delegating isn't something we do to completely clear our plates of work; it's a strategy that finds the right person for a task and frees up our time for more important work. Work that we can and should be doing includes: having effective 1:1s, building relationships across partner teams and across the company, gaining a deeper understanding of what's happening in other parts of the company so that we can find opportunities to collaborate, looking for stretch projects for our team members, finding visibility opportunities for our team members…there's no shortage of options. These are the leadership activities that we will finally have time to focus on when we get our heads above water.

Delegating myth #6: "My team isn't ready…" (Aaaaand we've found the biggest barrier: not fully trusting them!)

- **Solution:** Give them a small thing to do so that you can build confidence in their ability to take on something bigger.

To get a little more comfortable busting these myths when it comes to delegating, let's try a quick exercise.

Quick Exercise

What do I mean by delegating? We can sum it up in three easy steps.

- **Step 1:** Think of a piece of work that you can hand off to a team member, and list out any considerations or context that would be helpful for them to have. These considerations clarify why something is important, instead of feeling nitpicky.
- **Step 2:** In one of your 1:1 meetings, delegate that task. Set clear expectations regarding what they need to do, when you want to check in, and what success looks like.
- **Step 3:** HAND IT OFF AND LET IT GO.

Example

Step 1:

"I'd love for you to take over the preparation of an important executive presentation for the Q2 planning meeting. The main considerations are that this executive likes to see everything in Slides as opposed to PowerPoint so that they can easily add comments with questions, and they really like to dive into details. Make sure to have an appendix with all the supporting graphs and numbers so that we have everything in one place and can jump back and forth from the main presentation to the appendix."

Step 2:

"Let's meet on Wednesday to review progress so that you can email the slides to the meeting attendees by Friday morning. Success for this project means getting everyone's updates into the slide presentation on time and sending the completed slides to the attendees by Friday at 12 p.m."

Step 3:

"Go ahead and run with it, and we'll check in on Wednesday!"

Through our 1:1 meetings and career conversations, the work we've invested in getting to know our team members and their short- and long-term goals will give us a good sense of what we can delegate and whether they'll be ready to take something on.

Pro tip for delegating: Connect the task you are handing off to a career goal your team member has. Using the example from the exercise of preparing an executive presentation, tell your team member that *you've been looking for opportunities to get them more executive-level visibility and have identified this task as a great place to start.* Doing so will help them be so much more eager to take on that piece of work.

One more thing about delegating: it doesn't only require offloading the task at hand; it also involves managing up (or setting expectations with your own manager). Years ago, I was managing a team member who was responsible for running an event that I had run the prior year. She loved producing events, whereas event planning is the bane of my existence, so it was the perfect thing to delegate. The problem was because it was a high-profile project and our VP wanted what felt like *real-time updates*, my manager was constantly checking in and asking for details about where things stood. Those inquiries made me feel like I had to get more involved in the weeds, even though my team member was totally handling it.

My team member started to get frustrated and asked if I didn't trust her to handle the project. At that moment, I realized I had to establish some boundaries with my own manager. I set up a meeting and told them I had handed off the event production to my team member because it was totally in her wheelhouse, and we had agreed to check in on progress every Wednesday. I asked my manager if it would work to give them an update each Wednesday. They said that would be fine, but there would be times when the VP might ask for an update outside of that schedule, in which case we'd have to be flexible. I was then able to relay to my team member that she might need to give more frequent updates from time to time, but not because I didn't trust her; it was because of the visibility of the project.

After those conversations, the worry over a lack of trust dissipated, and we were all able to work within the same established expectations about status updates. Managing up was key in this situation and gave my team member space to do a great job with the event.

Coaching

Like delegating, coaching is another tool that frees up our time to focus on the right things, while empowering our team members to step up and solve problems on their own. Coaching is about helping people find the answer to a question or the solution to a problem themselves. As managers, we act as accountability partners for them to reach the desired result.

In the same way a sports coach doesn't run out onto the field, grab the ball, and play the sport on behalf of their team member if they're about to mess something up, neither should we as managers. Every time we step in more than we need to, we take time away from other things we could be focusing on and prevent our team members from learning how to be self-sufficient in the future.

When we're playing the game for them, no wonder we don't have any time!

Tool

One of the most important coaching skills is listening. I don't mean listening for a break in the conversation so that you can interject with your point; I mean listening on a deeper level.

Many coaching frameworks map out three levels of listening that show up in a conversation:

- **Level 1:** listening to respond
- **Level 2:** listening to have a back-and-forth conversation
- **Level 3:** listening to what isn't being said (e.g., body language, tone, energy)

In pretty much *all* circumstances, we want to stay in Levels 2 and 3: listening with curiosity so that we can have an engaged conversation while also staying present to the body language or signals we might be receiving beyond the words themselves.

Level 3 listening allows us to go deeper with our teams and ask better questions to understand how they are feeling.

Someone slumping in their chair, looking at the floor, and saying, "Yeah, it's fine," when you assign them a new project is actually telling you: "It's very much *not* fine." This doesn't mean we pry, but we don't just think, *Phew, glad they didn't pull me into whatever mess is going on over there*, and move on. We say, "I'm here when you need me, and let's check in tomorrow just to make sure."

Another coaching tool is asking open-ended questions, often referred to as "powerful questions." Powerful questions begin with "what" or "how," never "why." While "what" and "how" get us thinking expansively about possibilities, "why" puts us on the defensive and into analysis mode. Coaching looks forward rather than backward. While some context can be helpful, the overanalysis that "why" questions can surface often keeps us stuck.

Can you think of an answer to the question "Why didn't that project go well?" that will *not* surface defensiveness? Not really. It throws the door wide open for finger-pointing, shame, and blame. This is a little trap I like to call "I'm dumb; they're wrong" or "I'm wrong; they're dumb"—works both ways!

But reframe that to "What might you do next time?" and the accountability stays in their court. Now they're looking toward the future instead of staying in the past.

Tool

Here are a few examples of powerful questions:

- What else is possible?
- What might be going on with the other person?
- What might you try next?
- What do you want from here?
- How might you approach this in the future?

Funny story: I was running a training and shared the tip to reframe questions from "why" to "what." One of the questions someone came up with to ask a team member was: "What was going through your head during this meeting?" Mmmmm close, but no.

The idea here isn't to slap a "what" onto a question and call it a day. Here's a less judgy option: "What was your thought process?"

Honestly, it's still pretty judgy, but I've been called hypersensitive more than once. Another alternative: "What's your perspective on this?" There we go. So much better.

To show you the magic of powerful questions, I ran a scenario through an AI tool to illustrate how you could have an entire conversation just by asking powerful questions. I'm not saying this approach won't irritate a team member, but it gives you a sense of how questions can really serve to move a conversation forward:

    Manager: Good morning, Sarah. How's the project coming along?

Sarah:	Hi, Mark. To be honest, I'm feeling pretty stuck. I've hit a roadblock with the data analysis portion, and I'm not sure how to proceed.
Manager:	I see. What's your perspective on the situation?
Sarah:	Well, the data set is much larger and more complex than I anticipated. I'm worried I might not have the right skills to handle it effectively.
Manager:	What possibilities do you see for addressing this challenge?
Sarah:	Hmm...I suppose I could try breaking it down into smaller chunks. Or maybe look for some advanced analysis techniques online?
Manager:	Those sound like interesting ideas. What else comes to mind?
Sarah:	I guess I could also reach out to the data science team for advice. They might have some insights or tools I haven't considered.
Manager:	How might that impact your approach to the project?
Sarah:	It could give me a fresh perspective and potentially save me a lot of time if they have experience with similar data sets.
Manager:	What's holding you back from taking that step?
Sarah:	I'm a bit hesitant to ask for help. I don't want to seem incompetent or like I can't handle my own projects.
Manager:	How else could you view asking for assistance?
Sarah:	I suppose it could be seen as taking initiative and being resourceful. It might even lead to some valuable connections within the company.
Manager:	What would be the ideal outcome of this situation for you?

Sarah:	Ideally, I'd find a way to efficiently analyze the data and complete the project on time, while also expanding my skills in the process.
Manager:	How can you move closer to that ideal outcome?
Sarah:	I think I'll start by reaching out to the data science team for advice, and then create a plan to tackle the analysis in smaller, more manageable steps.
Manager:	What's your first step going to be?
Sarah:	I'll draft an email to the data science team lead right after this meeting, explaining my situation and asking if someone could spare some time to discuss the project.
Manager:	How confident do you feel about this plan?
Sarah:	Actually, I'm feeling much better about it now. Thanks for helping me think it through!
Manager:	What have you learned from this conversation that you can apply to future challenges?
Sarah:	I've realized that sometimes just talking through a problem can help me see new solutions. And that it's okay to seek help when I need it—it's actually a strength, not a weakness.

Pretty wild, right?! Can you start to see how we could bring our teams a ton of clarity simply by asking questions?

Why This Works

When I spoke at a conference recently, an audience member asked me what they should do if a team member was about to make a big mistake with something they'd just delegated. Should they stay out of it and let the team member learn the big lesson?

My response was that it depends on the consequence of making that mistake. If there's a client or financial impact (which, honestly, is probably the case in most situations), the approach should be somewhere in the middle.

Tool

When you see a problem brewing with something you've delegated, take these steps:

1. **Instead of leaving it as a "sink or swim" situation, first ask the team member whether they see the issue you're predicting. Maybe they were about to get to it, and you just happened to see it slightly earlier. In this case, they can continue running with the project.**
2. **If they didn't see the problem or aren't sure how to move forward, it's a great opportunity for them to shadow you. Explain what you saw and how you'd go about preventing or resolving it, bringing them along in the process.**

Be mindful not to just take over and say you'll handle it while they go do something else. This is a valuable learning opportunity for them to be able to avoid that issue the next time.

Coaching Skills in Action

In one of our routine 1:1s, a team member once came to me and said, "I've been on the team for three years. It's time I got a promotion. I need you to get it for me."

Naturally, I was taken aback for a number of reasons.

Chapter 6

First, "it's time" isn't a justification I've ever heard work for a promotion, especially when it's not paired with any proof points around results delivered. Then there was the "I need you to get it for me part," as though I was just sitting on this secret power of granting promotions and simply by saying the magic words, this person would receive one. In actuality, a committee of managers determined promotions, based on sustained performance operating at the next level of hierarchy in the company.

The approach I needed to take to help this team member was *not* to give her a checklist of all of the things she needed to do to get promoted. With the decision not being fully in my control, even if I thought I knew exactly what she needed to do, there was no guarantee of the outcome. Plus, giving someone a list doesn't mean they'll follow it in the way I envisioned. Let's say she followed the list to a tee and didn't get the promotion—all of a sudden it's my fault for providing her with the wrong guidance? Nope, I'll steer clear of that.

Instead, I leaned on my coaching skills and suggested she do the following:

> "Talk to three or four people who recently got promoted, and ask them what they did to go from the level of hierarchy you are at to the next one—who did they build relationships with, what kinds of challenges did they take on, and what visibility did their work need? Then, take a look back through the work you've done over the past six months and at what's on deck next, and identify any gaps, being really honest with yourself. Come back to me with a proposal for what to focus on to get to the next level, and I'll give you feedback on the plan."

By putting the ball in her court, I ensured she came back to me with a plan that *she* felt accountable and responsible for. I gave her feedback and ideas for where to dial up some of her efforts so that I could advocate more strongly in the manager committee for her promotion, but again, I never promised it was in the bag.

As she worked away on the plan, she felt excited about it because she had put it together, and her work performance increased dramatically. When she received her promotion the following cycle, it wasn't because it was time or because I had gotten it for her; it was because she had made a plan and stayed accountable for it.

Delegating and Coaching Don't Put Us Out of a Job

When your team is kicking butt, no one looks at you and thinks, "The team is awesome, but gosh, I really wonder what that manager even does here?" People immediately assume (and frankly expect) the manager has a role in that success.

Why? Because you better believe that if a team is floundering, people know the manager sucks.

Delegating helps *us* scale. Instead of always being in the same meetings as your team members, consider:

- What would it look like to delegate certain parts of the things you talk about in those meetings to other team members?
- What expectations can you set about how you want to be kept informed so that you do feel comfortable handing those things off?
- What is the right level of context needed for them to represent your team effectively, without throwing in the kitchen sink?

Chapter 6

Think back to our sports team analogy—it is *impossible* to do well if you have a bad coach, right? Great coaches spend time in practices and in all of their interactions ensuring that their teams are as prepared as possible to go out there and win games on their own.

When I was waiting on the decision regarding my team member's promotion, for a moment, I wondered if I had left it too much in her court—was there more I could have done? But when I learned that she'd gotten it, I knew my approach of coaching her as opposed to giving her a recipe (that may or may not have turned out well) was the right one to take. Months later when I shared I was moving on to a new team, she told me I was one of her favorite managers. She said it was because I helped her feel in control of her career, instead of like she was always waiting for things to happen.

When our team members are frustrated, it's easy to think we can make everything better by solving their problem for them. But instead of just taking away the problem, we take away their sense of accomplishment when *they* solve it.

When we teach our teams how to fish and rise to their full potential, the benefits pay off tenfold. Not only do we free up time to actually *lead* instead of staying bogged down in the weeds, we also motivate our team members by showing them they are capable of so much more than they realized.

How to keep this motivation strong even amid change and uncertainty is what we'll talk about next.

"TRUE LEADERSHIP IS ABOUT EMPOWERING OTHERS TO SEE THEIR POTENTIAL AND IGNITING A PASSION FOR EXCELLENCE. FOR EXAMPLE, IN THE HOME BUILDING INDUSTRY, EVERY DETAIL MATTERS, AND IT'S THE CREATIVITY AND DEDICATION OF THE TEAM THAT TRANSFORMS A VISION INTO REALITY. I INSPIRE MY TEAM BY REMINDING THEM THAT REGARDLESS OF THEIR ROLE, THEIR WORK CREATES SPACES WHERE MEMORIES ARE MADE, AND THEIR PASSION IS WHAT TURNS HOUSES INTO HOMES. THIS IS THE ULTIMATE FUEL FOR MOTIVATION, EVEN DURING CHALLENGING TIMES."

—Chris Hartley,
Area President at K. Hovnanian Homes

Chapter 7
Motivation Your Team to Excel

And can we not advertise how little work we're doing?

The first time I heard about "quiet quitting," I thought to myself, Well that can't be a good idea—employees advertising on TikTok that they barely do anything at work?

Quiet quitting took on a life of its own for multiple reasons. Workers were reclaiming boundaries, bringing to light the fact that many people were unhappy and disengaged in their work, and signaling that something needed to be done about it.

All good things.

But I believe there was also a major unforeseen consequence within companies large and small: it planted seeds of justification to the powers that be that they should conduct layoffs because people were LITERALLY MAKING VIDEOS ON THE INTERNET TALKING ABOUT HOW THEY DIDN'T DO ANY WORK.

My antidote to quiet quitting is actually the same as my strategy for retaining team members: checking in with them proactively, giving feedback, and recognizing their work. This gives us a ton of insight into how they're feeling about the job in general because, like it or not, keeping your team feeling motivated is one of your responsibilities as a manager.

Where We Get Stuck

There are a lot of people who come to work, get their jobs done, and don't really expect more from it. Frankly, those people make your job pretty easy as a manager. They roll with the punches, take on a little extra work when someone needs to pick up some slack, and are generally content with what they're doing.

If this describes your team, then you're lucky to have been dealt a relatively easy hand of cards.

If this describes *you* but not your team, then you're likely to be pretty confused as to why people won't just go with the flow.

And if this describes you *and* your team, and your company leadership puts more pressure on you to deliver results, you might find it even harder to motivate people to go above and beyond in their jobs.

More and more, I'm seeing that people want, well, *more* from their jobs. It's not just about a paycheck; we want to be appreciated, we want to be seen, and—okay, fine—we want a bigger paycheck.

In my consulting and coaching sessions these days, both managers and nonmanagers tell me all the time, "I'm just not motivated."

Chapter 7

Hearing this statement as a manager, especially when your teams are being paid well, you might want to throw up your hands and say, "How the hell is that *my* problem?"

It *is* your problem—because if your team isn't motivated, they're likely to be less productive and their job performance will start to suffer.

It's even more of your problem as people start venting to each other about how they're not motivated, fanning the flames of job dissatisfaction across the team.

In that scenario, you start feeling even less motivated as a manager and wondering how you got stuck dealing with all of this. It's a lose-lose.

Try This Instead

When it comes down to it, people are motivated by different things. As I discussed in Chapter 1, culture, upbringing, age, and other dimensions of identity all play a role. A common generalization for GenZ is that they're motivated by "purpose over purse strings."

At first, this idea might feel overwhelming, like *How am I supposed to give my team a sense of purpose?* That is until you realize that as a first-time manager, you don't have a ton of control over the purse strings anyway.

The reality is we have a lot more influence over fueling a sense of purpose than we might think.

In Chapter 3, I mentioned the 2015 study that Google conducted to find the secret sauce behind high-performing teams. Psychological safety was the leading indicator, but there was more to the story.

Along with psychological safety, there were four other qualities that showed up on high-performing teams: dependability (that sense of accountability we talked about), structure and clarity (clear expectations—seeing a trend here?), meaning, and impact.

We fuel a sense of purpose by understanding what is meaningful to our team members about their jobs and showing them that their work matters.

Many managers worry that if the company they work for isn't on a mission to end world hunger, they can't do anything to foster a sense of meaning and impact. Don't sell your team members short. People find meaning in all sorts of things—helping other colleagues be successful, learning a new skill, overcoming a fear or challenge, solving complex problems.

We help our team members find this meaning by getting to know their interests, passions, superpowers, and career aspirations. That doesn't mean we have to shape their whole job around those dimensions, but by knowing what they are, we can figure out creative ways to weave them in where it makes sense.

Understanding our teams' interests and passions helps everyone connect on a deeper level. For example, I belonged to a team where at each of our weekly meetings, someone would get ten minutes to teach something related to one of their hobbies or interests. One person taught the group how to quickly edit a photo in Photoshop, another how to start a fire if you're out in the wilderness. We all had so much fun learning these new things every week and saw a whole new side of our team members, fueling a sense of empathy and helping us to assume best intentions when the hard stuff came up.

Understanding superpowers and career aspirations helps us find opportunities for our team members to play to their strengths and get into a flow state. For example, if we know they are great relationship builders, we could put them in a situation where they have to build alignment across multiple teams, both leaning in to their strengths and allowing them to take on more leadership responsibility.

Quick Exercise

Write down the names of your team members, and then for each one, list three of their strengths or superpowers and one of their career goals. If you don't know what these are, make it a mission to find out over the course of your next two to three 1:1 meetings.

<u>Team Member 1</u>
Strength/superpower:
Strength/superpower:
Strength/superpower:
Career goal:

<u>Team Member 2</u>
Strength/superpower:
Strength/superpower:
Strength/superpower:
Career goal:

Team Member 3

Strength/superpower:
Strength/superpower:
Strength/superpower:
Career goal:

Showing your team members how their work connects to the bigger picture will help them see the impact of their work.

Example

Team Member: *John Snow*
Strength/superpower: *Great dot connector, always sees the bigger picture*
Strength/superpower: *Explains complex ideas with simplicity*
Strength/superpower: *Livens the energy in the room, gets people excited about ideas*
Career goal: *Becoming a VP of Marketing*

Download a template for this at liagarvin.com/playbook-resources.

When I was managing program managers, my direct reports would often say they thought their work was too administrative and tactical. It was the kind of role that people didn't notice when things were going well; they were only visible when things went badly. Once, one of my team members even referred to herself as a "task babysitter" or "professional nag."

When I heard this, I knew I had to step in and connect the dots—she wasn't seeing the bigger impact of her work.

Chapter 7

"I gotta stop you right there," I said, "and it's not just because I spent a decade working as a program manager and think that's the worst possible way to talk about the work. Do you want to know how I see this role and your role on our team? You are a strategic partner to your design, engineering, and product partners—forming the connective tissue across the departments, understanding the bigger picture, foreseeing risks, and charting the course to get an incredibly complex project with competing priorities and demands done on time. How in the world is that a 'professional nag'?"

With this framing, she realized she was looking at the job too narrowly; when it came to what was possible with her role, she wasn't seeing the forest for the trees.

When our team members feel unmotivated, there's a good chance they're looking at their role through too narrow a lens.

In my interview with storytelling coach Alex Street in episode 29 of my podcast *Managing Made Simple*, he reminds us that leaders can inspire their teams to see the impact of their work through the power of storytelling. In his example about working at a department store to set up the makeup counter or fold pants, he says the job isn't selling pants:

> We are actually giving them [our customers] confidence to face their day, to feel like they look good. And if you look good, you feel good. If you feel good, you do good. Like there's this—you paint that story, and that is what goes out in your company-wide emails. That's what goes out in your Monday morning meeting. That's what we talk about, is I'm so grateful that you are here today for your eight-hour shift, because today, you're gonna give people confidence to go and live their lives better.

We might not all be Don Drapers like Alex, but we can all help our team members see that no matter what their specific job is, they are a part of something bigger than themselves.

> ## Quick Exercise
>
> Write down the names of your team members, and then for each one, list how their role fits into the company's larger mission or top priorities. For example, a project manager keeps projects on schedule so that team members can deliver the product or service on time. Without a project manager, the product or service would never reach the hands of the customers.
>
> <u>Team Member 1</u>
> Role:
> Connection to the bigger picture:
>
> <u>Team Member 2</u>
> Role:
> Connection to the bigger picture:
>
> <u>Team Member 3</u>
> Role:
> Connection to the bigger picture:
>
> *Example*
>
> **Team Member:** *John Snow*
> **Role:** *Marketing Manager*
>
> **Connection to the bigger picture:** *One of our topline priorities in the next twelve months is expanding our business in five new regions. With a deep understanding*

of our customers' goals and motivations, as well as the development of messaging campaigns targeted to address the needs of different global regions, the marketing manager plays a crucial role in our success in this expansion.

Download a template for this at liagarvin.com/playbook-resources.

Why This Works

Supporting our team members in accomplishing their goals, recognizing their work, and providing them with opportunities to grow and take on stretch opportunities are all incredibly powerful motivators—and they cost you nothing.

A survey by Indeed and the Forrester research company found that 57 percent of respondents felt like their employer was responsible for individuals' happiness at work, but only 50 percent believed that their company was actually *doing something* to improve employee well-being and happiness.[33]

We can motivate our teams by providing coaching and mentorship when they're reaching for new goals and building new skills. We can support them in finding training and professional development opportunities. We can encourage them to attend or speak at conferences. We can help them get more visibility with senior leaders across the company.

And remember, it doesn't just stop at the career-related stuff. Knowing managers support personal goals is also highly motivating for team members. I'm not suggesting you carve out time for someone's side hustle. But if someone on your team has a hobby they're really excited about—playing music, woodworking, or whatever it is—encourage them to share how it's going. Recognize there is a whole person there who has interests outside of work.

Paying people well will get them in the door—it might even keep them there when they hate their job—but pay alone isn't what's going to inspire them to do their *best* work. There's more to the equation.

Building friendships and having close relationships with colleagues play a big role in maximizing performance. While as the manager, *you* might not be central to that friend group, you can help facilitate friendships. A study about employee satisfaction conducted by Wiley, one of the most notable publishing companies for education-related books, found that 59 percent of respondents reported that having friends at work was one of the leading reasons they stayed at a company.[34]

Our team members want to feel connected to others; they want to be a part of something. And one way they build relationships with other people is when their manager creates the meaningful moments that enable them to connect. Organize team lunches, celebrate birthdays, share wins at team meetings—all of this motivates your team to invest more deeply than just completing their task list, creating that sense of ownership and personal accountability we talked about in Chapter 5.

People also want to feel like they're moving *toward* something. In Chapter 2, I talked about the situation of being "layered" when my new manager, James, joined my team. We often have to deal with this frustration when we're only one rung ahead of our team members on the ladder. In that situation, our teams can feel, just as I felt, that they've experienced a career setback. It can be unmotivating, and even tougher, they might resent us for stepping into the role—even though we had nothing to do with the decision.

But by walking the talk of amplifying my work instead of stifling it, and helping bring the visibility to my work that I wasn't getting, James ended up being one of my best managers. Being "layered" ended up resulting in my promotion.

How do you know all the effort you put into keeping your teams motivated is actually paying off? Motivated people show up to work differently. They aren't already "over it," the way so many people act these days the minute you ask them to do even the smallest thing. They're up for a challenge, ready to jump in and solve a problem, and okay if they have to do a little extra in a pinch, because they feel good about the work.

Retention is another indicator. When team members stay on the team, it's a *pretty strong signal* that they feel motivated.

Instead of feeling disempowered that you don't have the means to pay team members more because their salaries are legitimately not in your control, feel empowered that you can motivate them in countless other ways, while advocating to the higher-ups for financial incentives.

Doing so will pay off in spades.

It's a good thing, because there will be times when situations go sideways on the team and you'll rely on the motivation currency you've worked so hard to bank. You'll need to cash it in to navigate conflicts.

"PERSONAL CONFLICTS ARE ALWAYS A RELATIONSHIP BREAKDOWN. AND SO IT NEEDS TO BE SOLVED WITH A CONVERSATION. YOU HAVE TWO OPTIONS REALLY: YOU CAN EITHER TALK TO EACH PERSON INDIVIDUALLY AND TRY TO BE THE MIDDLEMAN ON HOW TO SOLVE THE PROBLEM, OR COACH THEM ON HOW TO HAVE THE CONVERSATION THEMSELVES, WHICH TRULY IS THE BEST THING FOR YOU TO COACH YOUR EMPLOYEE."

—Jackie Koch,
CEO of People Principles,
Fractional Recruiting and HR Consulting

Chapter 8
Conflict Management

Navigating the stickiest situations... of which there are many

Someone reached out to me for help with their situation as a manager in their company. They said they were working for a very controlling boss and had been made the manager of someone who was older than they were—oh, and this person was their boss's mom.

Yikes, I thought to myself, *that is a doozy to say the least.*

When we first become managers, we want things to go smoothly. We want the high-performing team members who find motivation within themselves, look for places to go above and beyond, are open to feedback, and always work to improve, but not in an obnoxious way—in other words, we want unicorns.

Right?

Hey, we want this whether we're new to managing or not.

Yet the majority of the time, there's some kind of dynamic on our team that makes even the most ideal situation hard. And if it goes well for a while, one day out of nowhere, your star team member leaves to pursue their passion as a modern-art sculptor. Then there you go—your house of cards starts to crumble.

Where We Get Stuck

As managers, we face no shortage of sticky situations, many of which we have no idea how to handle. Or we have a really good idea of how we'd *want* to handle them, but we don't want to get fired in the process.

Hate to tell ya, but if you're afraid of conflict, you're in the wrong job.

I'm not saying you have to run toward conflict with open arms, but you can't be effective at managing if you head for the hills (or to HR) every time a conversation doesn't go as well as planned.

When we're new managers, conflict can be intimidating. In trying to make it go away or resolve it as quickly as possible, we can fall into the trap of "solving" something that's not even the issue. Usually this means getting involved where we shouldn't or taking sides where we shouldn't. Alternatively, we might do nothing at all when we should do *something* to help move the situation toward resolution.

Conflict can be time-consuming. Remember that 65 percent gap between how managers perceive their teams to be doing and how employees report they are doing? I've got to believe that some managers are saying they think everything is fine on their teams just to avoid looking behind the curtain.

We also avoid conflict because we genuinely feel ill-equipped.

If my team member says they're unhappy with their job, what the hell am I supposed to do about that?

What if they say they have too much work? It's not like my boss is going to ease up.

As middle managers, we may feel powerless, so we don't really want to hear about the truth.

Try This Instead

Love it or hate it, conflict *is* going to show up on your teams at some point. Let's prepare for it by understanding what is actually going on so that we can figure out the best solution.

Tool

Conflict on teams typically falls into four general categories:

1. Conflict between your team member and their *role or scope of work*

   a. <u>What this looks like:</u> A team member comes to you saying they're overwhelmed or unmotivated, they don't have enough time to finish things, or they are generally dissatisfied with their role.

   b. <u>What to do:</u> Ask follow-up questions like "What does 'overwhelmed' mean to you?" or "What's the biggest frustration right now?" to uncover the root of the issue. Is it the scope of work as a whole, the expectations you've set, the difficulty of the task or skill level required, the timeline, the budget, or something else? Each of these factors will take you in a completely different direction to reduce overwhelm, so you don't want to start solving until you better understand what is *actually* happening for this person.

2. Conflict between your team member and *you*

a. <u>What this looks like:</u> They have an attitude or air of irritation when they talk to you, they say "yes" to things but the body language doesn't match, or they say "yes" but don't follow through.

b. <u>What to do:</u> Ask for feedback and *listen* with an open mind. Resist getting defensive even if you don't like what you're hearing. Are they frustrated because they think feedback you recently shared with them was unwarranted? Reset expectations around whatever the feedback was about or bring in more specific examples. Is it about your management style? Talk about what doesn't resonate—too direct, too indirect, something else? Is it that they think you can't help them achieve their career goals? Talk about what those specific goals are, and make a plan for what *each of you* (not just you) will do to help them achieve those.

3. Conflict between your team member and a *peer*

a. <u>What this looks like:</u> They constantly come to you complaining about another team member and do not take responsibility for their own role in any of the issues. They might ask you to take action or imply that they will leave the team if you don't fix it.

b. <u>What to do about it:</u> Get the two people talking to each other. While it can feel like you're being helpful at first, and your team members might *really really* want you to be the go-between, getting in the middle of a conflict only results in a longer game of telephone with even more assumptions and misunderstandings. My friend Jackie Koch, CEO of People Principles, Fractional Recruiting and HR Consulting, summarized it best in her interview on the *Earn Your Happy* podcast, quoted at the beginning of this chapter. She goes on to say that as the team leader, not only do you need to suggest that the two team members speak directly, you also have to follow up and hold them accountable for actually doing it, since they'll likely try to avoid it.[35]

4. Conflict between your team member and another *team*

a. <u>What this looks like:</u> A narrative of "us versus them" has emerged, and an individual or the whole team is feeling stuck or blocked because another team did or didn't do something.

b. <u>What to do about it:</u> Meet with the manager of the other team to talk about shared goals and align your working relationship. Avoid getting sucked into the "us versus them" mentality—you never know when a reorg will happen, and the "thems" become your team members or vice versa. If you've engaged in the drama, it will be super awkward. *Aaaaaand* participating in that kind of conflict is not showing up as a mature leader. Also that.

Managing Former Peers

While each of these categories has its challenges, I'll spend a little more time on managing former peers and friends, because that's where many new managers start.

In Chapter 1, I shared a story about managing my former friend Mindy. To cut to the chase, here are all of the places I went wrong when it came to shifting my relationship with her from friends to a manager and direct report:

- I told Mindy that even though I was her manager, nothing would change.
- We never had a conversation about what our new working relationship would look like.
- I never talked to my own manager about how this new dynamic would change communication.
- I didn't give Mindy early feedback when things weren't going well.
- I allowed problems to simmer until they boiled over.

I probably made more missteps as well, but those are the most glaring ones.

Needless to say, the right way to handle a transition like this is the inverse of what I did. I'll spell out the better approach in a few steps so that you can try it on your own.

Tool

When managing a former friend or peer, do the following:

1. Meet *right away* to talk about the fact that you're starting a *new* relationship and to agree that you will both approach it differently.
2. Talk explicitly about how you will give feedback (both positive and constructive), have hard conversations, discuss money, and so on. If there's anything that could come up and make things awkward, talk about it here.
3. Check in over the first few weeks to discuss how the shift is going, sharing any feedback you have and asking for feedback from your former friend or peer.
4. Don't downplay your role as the leader of the team in an effort to make the other person feel better or show them you're not on your high horse with the new manager title. Instead, talk about what you are excited about as a leader, your vision for approaching the work, and how you plan to help the team achieve their career goals. (This is the same stuff we talked about in Chapter 2 around setting intentions.)

You might think you and this person already know how to approach these issues from being friends, but the reality is, you don't. The manager-to-report relationship has a completely different dynamic than peer-to-peer; you are no longer equals. You have to talk about the plan out loud and reiterate it, even if doing so feels redundant.

Managing Someone Older than You

At the start of this chapter, I mentioned the tricky situation of managing someone significantly older than you. To address this situation, first I encourage you to think about how it might feel from your team member's perspective.

They presumably have more experience and more time in the job than you do, and they potentially wanted the role of manager. Your promotion could feel like a slap in the face or like a career setback, similar to my reaction when I got "layered."

There are cases when this setup works out great—your team member *didn't* want to be the manager, is really happy in doing their current role, and recognizes that managing is different from being an individual contributor. As a result, they do not feel slighted by the situation.

Either way, this person does have more life experience, and that's not something to be discounted. We used to live in a world where the expertise of people senior to us was highly valued and coveted. Sadly, this reverence has become less and less prevalent, resulting in a lot of ageism in the workplace. The speed of technology and a desire to always work toward the next "new" thing means the perspectives of older employees often get ignored.

Be the manager who values these perspectives.

This doesn't mean abandoning your own point of view or downplaying your own experience. It also doesn't prevent you from ultimately making the decisions. But it *does* mean that you don't discount a perspective or write it off as outdated just because it comes from someone who belongs to an older generation.

Tool

My advice for managing someone older than you is to:

1. Recognize the experience of the team member who is older than you, leaning on them for context and insight.
2. Share your approach to the work and what you bring to the table. Talk about how you plan to integrate previous learnings, experiences, and ways of doing things from that team member and everyone else on the team, along with your vision for where the team is headed in the future.

The manager of a PR team in a large media company recently came to me for coaching on how to address this exact issue. She was asked to take on managing the team with the goal of leveling up and modernizing their approach to what was needed in today's market, essentially shifting from more traditional PR to social and influencer marketing, TikTok, etc. However, one member of the team had been there for fifteen years and had been driving the traditional PR efforts. My client didn't want to alienate or devalue this team member, but she was also specifically asked by her own leadership chain to shift directions.

I encouraged her to use this two-step approach, leaning on the tenured team member to give her a sense of the history, what worked, what hadn't, and ideas for what was next—while *also* sharing the charter for the team, the expertise she was excited to bring to the table, and how she'd build on the existing work while looking toward strengthening the company's position as a player in the market in the future.

When to Go to HR

Now, it wouldn't be right to talk about conflict without mentioning when to go to HR. I'm not an HR professional, but my friends and colleagues who work in HR tell me all the time that *most* issues brought to HR are actually things that the team manager could—and should—resolve. Employees often come to HR because they feel frustrated about their job expectations, are in conflict with another team member, or don't like their performance rating—all of which they should work through with their manager first. The more we set expectations, give thoughtful feedback, and make the path to promotion crystal clear and transparent, the less people will go to HR for these issues.

When a team member comes to you for something you feel is out of your depth, my advice is to go to your own manager first; they might have dealt with this situation before or have guidance. Then, if you both agree that it's more of an HR issue, of course you should go to HR.

My friend and HR executive Hanja Kahan suggests:

> Managers should come to HR when they need an unbiased take on tricky employee situations, navigating compliance, or when things get too complex to handle solo. And if there's even a hint of harassment or discrimination, HR should be your first call. Think of HR as your go-to partner for next-level solutions that keep your team and the company on track.

Why This Works

As humans, we're always on the hunt for homeostasis, making it tempting to jump to the fastest and seemingly easiest resolution when a conflict shows up. But when we move too fast into solution mode, we lose sight of the fact that we might be solving the *wrong* problem.

Let's expand on the example of a team member saying they're feeling overwhelmed, which falls under the first conflict type. Hearing someone say they are overwhelmed, you might think about what it means when *you* feel overwhelmed: too much work on your plate, overly aggressive deadlines, too many meetings to attend. With this in mind, you might start shifting work to another team member in an effort to balance the load, because this action would provide immediate relief if you felt overwhelmed.

But if you stop to ask your team member how this overwhelm is showing up for them or what they think is causing it, they might say something like, "Ugh, my roommate moved out, and I've been interviewing new roommates almost every night these past few weeks. I'm really nervous I'm going to have to cover the rent all by myself if I don't find someone. It's funny—coming to work is the *only thing* that takes my mind off of how overwhelmed I am with the whole situation."

In that situation, taking work off of their plate would be the *last* thing they want. You would only know this, though, if you asked a deeper question to understand the root cause before jumping in with the problem-solving. If they get paid an hourly wage, they might actually want to take on *more* hours to give them some relief on paying the full rent.

Deeper questions asking "what" or "how" (examples below) are essentially the coaching "powerful questions" we talked about in Chapter 6 and will work wonders for gaining clarity on any of the conflict types.

Tool

Here are starter questions to pair with each of the conflict types to help you decide how to proceed:

1. **Conflict between your team member and their *role or scope of work***
   a. How is this showing up for you?
   b. What do you need right now?
   c. What does success look like?
2. **Conflict between your team member and *you***
   a. What is showing up for you right now?
   b. What's getting in the way?
   c. What is important to you?
3. **Conflict between your team member and a *peer***
   a. What might be going on with the other person?
   b. Where are you getting stuck?
   c. What else is possible?

Conflict between your team member and another *team*
   a. What would a best-case scenario look like?
   b. What might be most important to them?
   c. What might you try?

Each of these questions will get your team members thinking more expansively and pull them out of the defensive finger-pointing zone. Oftentimes, simply thinking through these questions defuses a conflict because they pull us out of victim mode and into action and accountability.

Chapter 8

For situations where the conflict arises out of a change in a dynamic or relationship, recognizing and naming the change breaks down the assumptions we're making and gives both parties an opportunity to reset.

I'll say it again: when it comes right down to it, all conflicts arise out of misaligned expectations. What's interpreted as disrespect is often a miscommunication; one person thought the expectation was one thing, and the other thought it was something else.

Staying Neutral

Looking at the four conflict types and what to do about them, what's the thread that connects all of them? *You* have to stay out of the middle.

Nothing gets resolved when you get sucked in and start taking sides. As the manager, maintaining a level of nonattachment is critical to your success.

Nonattachment is not apathy; it's keeping a healthy level of distance. InsightTimer, the popular meditation app, describes it as "not getting overly attached to desires, outcomes, material things, or self-concepts, allowing for a more flexible and open interaction with life. This approach fosters inner freedom, peace, and well-being by minimizing the suffering caused by clinging to specific expectations or fears."[36]

This lens allows us to stay at the right level of altitude, not feed into the drama, and not get thrashed by the highs and lows that naturally come with the job.

For me, a regular meditation practice, even five to ten minutes a day, has been really helpful to maintain a level of nonattachment in my work.

The Covey exercise I talked about in Chapter 2, identifying what's in your control versus what you can influence, is another useful tool that can give us some perspective.

I used to get really sucked in and overly emotionally invested when my team members were frustrated or when they asked me for help with something. Years ago, I had been spending extra time meeting with one team member, coaching them on how to be a more effective program manager, and really going above and beyond from a time and energy perspective. After about a month of this, I started noticing my team member wasn't implementing *anything* we talked about each week.

I shared my frustration with my own manager, and she replied with words that still stick with me today: "You can't care more than they care."

Sometimes we will try to help our team members through a challenge, and they won't be ready for it. That's not about *us*; it's about them.

You can't care more than they care.

Give all your team members the support and guidance they need to reach their goals, but save the extra energy for the ones who meet you halfway and show up ready to act.

Chapter 8

Remember, conflict will arise whether you like it or not; it comes with the territory.

But in building the skills we've talked about chapter by chapter, you should have laid enough of a foundation with your team to nip conflicts in the bud, before they get unwieldy.

With more confidence in your ability to resolve conflict, it won't feel scary to expand your team, which happens to be what we'll talk about next.

"THE DAYS, WEEKS, AND MONTHS OF A NEW JOB ARE AMONG THE MOST EXCITING AND ANXIOUS PERIODS OF OUR LIVES. REALIZING THAT THIS EXPERIENCE IS VERY COMMON FOR NEW EMPLOYEES, A LEADER THAT PRIORITIZES EMPATHY WILL CREATE A CULTURE OF SUPPORT AND CARE. A HAPPY AND COMFORTABLE NEW EMPLOYEE WILL BE ABLE TO MORE EFFECTIVELY GET TO THE 'WORK OF WORKING,' EAGER TO POSITIVELY IMPACT THEIR NEW TEAM."

—Marvin Stickel,
Global Talent Sourcing Director at Nike

Chapter 9
Hiring and Onboarding

Expanding your team thoughtfully

"I don't know what to do—I hired all the wrong people. Now I'm underwater, and there's nothing I can do about it," Steve said to me with a look of nausea, exhaustion, and a little bit of terror on his face.

He was running a marketing team and had lost three of his five team members in a matter of weeks. In an effort to maintain the aggressive workload and milestones his team was committed to, he hired two people quickly, without doing a ton of due diligence. I mean, what choice did he have? He couldn't get the work done with two people. Two mediocre team members couldn't sink the whole ship, right?

Wrong.

Steve came to me because his team wasn't delivering, even on the basics. He was stuck in the weeds with *everything:* mapping out how every project would get done (even when a project was the same as the last one), double-checking all work, and hand-holding for even the smallest, most cut-and-dried decisions.

In the fast-paced world of marketing, he'd hired people who weren't committed to keeping up with the speed required to hit the timelines.

It was a mess.

"What was your hiring and onboarding process?" I asked Steve.

He hesitated for a moment and then said, "I mean, we were so underwater—I just needed to get people in the door. I hired the first people who applied, and they just started working on stuff."

And I knew exactly where to begin.

Where We Get Stuck

We usually start the hiring process when there is an immediate need to fill. We're three points down, the shot clock is almost up, and we've got to shoot the ball from half-court. When we don't approach hiring and onboarding *thoughtfully*, it's like we pick up the basketball and drop-kick it into the bleachers.

Of course it makes sense why we'd want to rush hiring and onboarding, when the alternative is missing deadlines, overloading our existing team members, or having to fill the gaps ourselves. However, that doesn't mean we should.

The cost of *not* having the right people on the team—people who can hit the ground running, do the job, and bring the right energy and attitude to the work—is almost *always* higher than taking a beat to figure out how to hire the right person. Getting it wrong costs us more time in the end.

Steve's story is one I have heard dozens of times. The panic we feel when losing team members and still having a mountain of work to do clouds our decision-making, leading us to overlook red flags or bring on team members who aren't a good fit. Then, because we can't even come up for air, we don't onboard them effectively, throwing them into a sink-or-swim situation—only to feel disappointed and even *more* stressed when they sink.

This is the consequence of moving too fast with hiring, without a clear sense of what we are even looking for. If you're in that hiring rat race, in the immortal words of Tyler Durden of *Fight Club*, I have to ask: "How's that working out for you?" Not well? Didn't think so.

Again, I totally understand why you'd get into that situation: you can't imagine going another day without this work being covered. But you create a whole new slew of problems for yourself, including but not limited to the following:

- Managing people who aren't the right fit for the job, causing them to feel frustrated and be unable to add the value you anticipated
- Decreasing productivity across the whole team because people are being pulled away from their primary responsibilities to pick up the slack for others
- Losing A-players from your team because they don't want to work with folks who aren't pulling their weight
- Burning yourself out from having to be involved in every detail and still fill a lot of the gaps

Last, but not least, if a person is completely not a fit and has no hope of doing the job well, you've opened the door on a real goober of a management challenge: now you have to manage this person *out* (if you've never had to do that, "manage out" means "fire them").

But not thinking through our hiring plan isn't the only place we go wrong. When we're hiring new team members and need them to ramp up quickly (which is always), it can be tempting to think the whole process will be easier if we bring on people who are exactly like us. Maybe we work in similar ways, or maybe it's someone we could see ourselves being friends with. New managers will often tell me they hire based on "vibe."

Then the person starts, and we realize we haven't fully assessed their capability in the role, because let's face it: the fact that we'd want to go out for drinks with someone doesn't mean they are the right fit for a job that requires a specific skill set.

I get why it's tempting to hire people who work the way you do. Out of the gate, it *is* easier to manage them.

I also get why it's tempting to hire someone you'd be friends with. It makes work more fun.

But neither of these qualities lead to the best work; in fact, diverse teams composed of people who think and work differently from each other lead to better results and higher performance.

Hiring is a *major* decision; you want to use concrete and objective criteria instead of gut feel and vibes. And, well, legally you *have to* use concrete and objective criteria instead of feels and vibes.

Now, hiring isn't the whole story here. We can hire right and still go wrong when it comes to onboarding. Yay!

Onboarding will always have a special place in my heart, given my experience with the world's worst process.

Chapter 9

About a year after I got married, I checked my spam folder, only to come across an email that I knew would forever change my life: "Hello from [Famous Tech Company]." Growing up in the Bay Area adjacent to Silicon Valley, I had always been interested in working in tech, but without a technical background, it didn't seem like it was in the cards for me. Seeing this email inviting me to interview for a role at the company's headquarters, I knew I'd found my big break.

I responded that I was interested, nailed the interviews, and got the job.

My husband was in school at the time, which meant I'd have to move to a new state, rent a second apartment, and take on a long-distance relationship basically as a newlywed. However, we agreed it was totally worth it; this was my dream job.

Flash forward to my first day: I arrived at the office buzzing with excitement, and the administrative assistant for the team met me in the lobby.

"Welcome to the team, Lia," she said. "Let me walk you to your office."

OMG, an office!!! I silently screamed to myself. *I really have made it.*

"Here we are. Grace isn't here today, so go ahead and get settled in, and let me know if you need anything."

I walked into my office. No laptop, no note from my manager, Grace—no nothing. I sat in that office from 8:15 a.m. to 5 p.m. with a feeling of dread building in the pit of my stomach.

No one cared that I was there. My manager couldn't be bothered to give any instructions or even send an email to say hello. Uprooting my life and moving there for the job felt like the biggest mistake of my life.

The Society for Human Resource Management reports that within the first six months, 90 percent of new hires decide whether they want to stay at a company for the long term.[37] I decided it was a "no" for me within the first six *hours*.

How we show up for our teams on their first day, in the first few weeks, and over the first few months can make or break *everything*.

Try This Instead

Often as new managers, we inherit a team. We might start managing people we know or have worked with already, or we might join a new team as the manager. In either case, as they said in my daughter's preschool when they passed out the apple slices for afternoon snack, "We get what we get, and we don't get upset."

Take the time to understand the skills, strengths, and growth areas for your team. This is where setting an intention, building results-based relationships, and establishing expectations all come into play as the immediate first steps.

Then, at some point, there comes a time when you'll have to add new people to the team.

Chapter 9

Hiring

The question I get most from managers when they are building their teams is "How do I hire great people?"

Let's make one thing clear: hiring is not a guarantee. Whenever you hire anyone, you are taking a risk. You can never fully predict whether someone will be a perfect fit.

If you were thoughtful about the process and hired someone who seemed awesome but didn't work out, it doesn't help to blame yourself and decide you're a terrible manager who sucks at hiring.

Quick Exercise

If you've hired someone in the past who wasn't a fit, take five minutes to reflect on these two questions:

- *Was it a skills gap?* In other words, did the person seem to have great potential but just didn't have the necessary skill set?
- *Was it a behavior mismatch?* In other words, did the person present in a certain way in the interviews but act differently, in a way that was not a fit, once they started on the team (e.g., they weren't open to feedback or were not a team player)?

The clearer and more specific we are about what didn't work out, the more we reduce bias toward hiring people who work the same way we do.

In addition, this clarity helps us identify which qualities we really *do* want new team members to bring to the table.

Another common mistake in hiring is bringing someone on for a highly specialized role, only to find this person doesn't have a home if priorities change down the line. Specialists are awesome in many cases, and if we hire them, it's also our responsibility to keep a line of sight open for what they might focus on if the work of the team shifts.

Before you start hiring, think about what it means to be a great member of your team. For example, do you want people who are:

- Open to feedback?
- Adaptable?
- Flexible?
- Generalists so that they can take more on as the team grows?
- Specialists so that they can accelerate speed in a specific area?

Really think about these parameters. Then ask yourself, *How can I suss out the answers to these questions in an interview?*

When we move too fast, we often don't leave enough time to figure out what we're really looking for or who would be the right fit. Instead, we want to cultivate a solid pipeline of options so that we can narrow them down to the best choice.

To be clear, I'm not talking about taking months and months to hire. Understand the qualities you are looking for in your ideal candidate *up front*, and make a list of the questions you will ask *all* candidates in order to give everyone an equitable opportunity. When you post the role, leave the job posting up for two weeks. This should give you sufficient time to be well set up for interviews.

Tool

Before you start talking to candidates, establish the criteria that you plan to use to evaluate everyone applying for that role.

Make a spreadsheet listing all the qualities you are evaluating for in the columns, with the names of the candidates in the rows.

As a candidate meets a criterion, put an X in that square. After your interviews, the people with the most boxes checked will be on the short list of folks who move to the final selection round.

Candidate	Experience Managing	Public Speaking	Writing Skills	Salesforce Experience	Notes
Alex	X	X	X		Great examples of being open to feedback
Chris		X	X	X	One of the strongest writing samples

Download a template at liagarvin.com/playbook-resources.

Onboarding

When it comes to onboarding, think of it as an experience you are creating for someone so that *right away* they think, "Wow, I am SO FREAKING GLAD I joined this team."

Spoiler: Good onboarding requires more than just sending a welcome email.

Tool

Here are a few ideas to create a successful onboarding process:

- Before the new team member's start date, mail a physical card or send an email to their personal email address (if you worked with a recruiter, ask the recruiter to ask the new hire for this information if they are comfortable sharing). Share how excited you are that they're joining the team, and explain what to expect during their first week.
- Create an onboarding checklist that outlines where new hires can learn about the team and find information about projects, whom to meet and connect with, etc. so that they have something concrete to reference and work through during their first few weeks.
- Share a list of team and company tips and norms, including typical start and end times for work, whether there's a "casual Friday" in the office, where folks typically eat lunch (e.g., in the cafeteria, bring from home, lunch spots in the area), how to use the fancy coffee machine, where to keep snacks and other

food, where the closest bathroom is, how to use the printer, etc. so that the team member doesn't feel like a fish out of water their first few days.
- Assign an onboarding buddy to proactively check in with the new team member throughout the week.
- Set up a team lunch on the first day or during the first week.
- Block off fifteen minutes at the end of each day of the new hire's first week to check in and answer questions.

None of these things take more than fifteen to twenty minutes to do! Isn't that worth creating a great experience for someone?

Download an example onboarding checklist at liagarvin.com/playbook-resources.

Part of onboarding is outlining what our expectations are for the first few weeks.

Consider:

- What do you expect them to know or be doing by the end of the first week? Week two? Month one?
- Do you want them to ramp up slowly and take things in for a while, or hit the ground running and start making decisions right away?
- Who is most important for them to connect with right away? Can you encourage people to prioritize making the time to meet with this new team member?

Being clear on the answers to these questions will set both of you up for success, reduce misunderstandings, and help the new team member get off to a great start.

One more thing to remember: onboarding isn't just for someone new to the team; it's also needed when someone changes roles. If a team member's role changes dramatically (e.g., they become a manager or switch from creative to operational), they are doing a *new* job and need to go through the respective onboarding process. In particular, it's important for them to understand expectations for the first few weeks or months. Discuss their thirty-, sixty-, and ninety-day plans, and facilitate introductions just as you would for a new member of your team.

Why This Works

Hiring and onboarding are your opportunities to curate your team or supplement the great people you already have with additional equally awesome people. It's also a chance to bring in more A-players who can elevate the performance of the whole team.

As I said at the start of the chapter, anytime you hire someone new, you are taking a risk. People can look pretty darn good on a résumé or show up great in an interview and then not pan out. But when we approach hiring methodically, really being clear on what we're looking for and how to assess it, we reduce that risk significantly.

And if you've ever been in a situation remotely similar to what Steve found himself in, or if reading that story sent a chill down your spine, then you see the benefits of being thoughtful about hiring and onboarding—and why taking that extra week or two is so worth it.

Chapter 9

When we hire well, our team morale is better, work productivity increases, and we personally don't have to stay in the weeds. We can operate at a more strategic level. Onboarding is a piece of good hiring; it creates a springboard to allow our new hires to be effective from day one.

My client Alecia, who heads up the client services function in an advertising agency, shared with me recently that she had hired someone for her team. Two weeks in, that team member came to her and said that she didn't feel like she was a fit for the role. While Alecia was relieved the team member came to this realization on her own (as opposed to it turning into a "manage out" situation), she couldn't help but wonder whether she could have set better expectations during the interviewing and onboarding stages.

My answer was *yes*.

The more up-front we are about our expectations, the more candidates can make an informed decision. Share insights on whatever would be useful to help someone determine whether they will be able to keep up in the new role: the pace you work at, the overall workload, whether people operate with a lot of direction or very little, etc. The more info, the better.

In interviews, frame these expectations in terms of what it looks like to succeed on the team, not as threats or warnings. For example:

> "In the advertising space, we move at a rapid pace, often having deadlines that can keep team members working late into the evenings. While we always make sure people

are compensated for extra time, the most successful team members are on board with this pace and flexible with working more during some weeks and less during others."

Certain industries lend themselves to a faster pace, and it can be frustrating as a manager to hire someone who doesn't realize that. It's also frustrating for new hires when they feel like they've been misled. People need to hear any expectations and considerations explicitly. Be transparent in the interview so that the candidate can decide whether to move forward with the role with their eyes wide open.

During the onboarding process, remind team members of what they've committed to. I have a number of clients who run businesses that require weekend work, and when taking a role in that company, team members commit to being available on the weekends. When managers don't reiterate this requirement right away, they often find team members resisting the weekend work when it comes up, even though they signed up for it.

The most excited your team members will ever be is in their first few weeks; capitalize on this energy from the moment they walk in the door. Maintain and sustain it by making sure your new hire is a great mutual fit and that their initial experience on your team is as seamless as possible.

Little things matter—asking them what their favorite coffee drink is and having that ready for them on their desk, setting up a team lunch for the first day so that they can start getting to know people, making sure to send that welcome email on the first day or two

Chapter 9

instead of three weeks in. These things show our teams we care about them and want them to be there—and that they're not an afterthought.

On one of my past teams, the manager, Rachel, would hand people a sponge when they first started. Paraphrasing here...

"Over the next few weeks, I want you to be a sponge. Learn as much as you can. Ask as many questions as you can. Just be new and take it all in. You're not expected to be delivering anything just yet—your job is to be a sponge," she said, encouraging new hires to keep the sponge on their desks as a reminder.

A lot of times in an effort to show their value, new team members come in hot. They share too many ideas and suggestions when they know little to nothing about the current team. As a result, they make a bad first impression, and it can take a while to get back on the right foot.

On the other hand, sometimes people take it too slow. Their new coworkers end up looking around like, "Is the new guy ever gonna actually do anything?"

Make the expectations clear, like Rachel did. If they're supposed to be a sponge, tell them. If they're supposed to fully immerse themselves and start delivering on something, tell them.

Tool

Meet with your teams at thirty, sixty, and ninety days in to talk about how things are going, answer questions, and give feedback.

Treat these as different meetings from your existing 1:1s. These meetings are specifically for checking in on how the role is going, and you might want to prepare different agenda items to talk about than in a 1:1.

Jackie Koch, the CEO of People Principles I mentioned in Chapter 8, recommends prescheduling these onboarding check-ins on the calendar so that someone doesn't see "90-Day Check-in" pop up on their calendar out of nowhere and think they're getting fired.

Bonus: Mention these meetings on your onboarding checklist as well!

Diverse Teams Drive Better Results

Hiring is your opportunity to build a team representative of the world around you, and doing that is one of your most important responsibilities as a manager. Diverse teams drive better results. Teams that consist of people from similar backgrounds, job histories, and life experiences can fall into the trap of "groupthink," where their similarities cause them to look at solving problems in the same way. Creativity and innovation are results of people with different perspectives looking at challenges through different lenses, which can uncover biases and assumptions.

There are countless instances of products, services, and experiences that have inadvertently excluded people from different backgrounds: for example, camera phones taking lower-quality pictures of people with darker skin[38] and gender bias in AI, including the recent example of ChatGPT showing a team of male executives when the woman CEO of Chanel asked for an image of Chanel's leadership team.[39]

While it is everyone's responsibility to be cognizant of potential biases in the products and services they are creating, with more diverse representation on your team, you increase the likelihood that people will anticipate and prevent these issues before they ever see the light of day. Double-check your job descriptions for language that might show bias toward or against certain groups (for example, research shows that words like "rockstar" and "ninja" can have gendered connotations[40]), leave job postings open for at least two weeks to cultivate a strong pipeline, and ask candidates the same interview questions (using the tool I shared earlier in the chapter) to ensure you are assessing them on the same criteria.

It's Worth the Effort

Even in the most stressful circumstances, I still believe that none of us have to feel the overwhelm and desperation that Steve felt when he came to me. Given that there are situations where you'll have to move fast in your hiring process, figure out the criteria you are looking for in new team members *in advance*, when you are not hiring and have time to think about it.

Continually collect feedback on your onboarding process to refine it and make it better. Then, when you have to move fast in the hiring, you've worked out the kinks and can quickly ramp someone up into the work, set expectations, and make the necessary connections to get them rolling.

And in those moments when you don't make the best call, give yourself some grace. Don't write it off as a lost cause if you feel like you made a bad decision; give that person a chance to course-correct. Working in team operations and program management for most of my career, I've found that even the best talent can be less effective if we don't have the right systems in place, if we don't set clear expectations, or if our processes are too clunky. If someone is off to a rocky start, consider: Is there something about how work currently flows through the team that makes it harder for people to be successful? Make it easier for people to get their work done, and you will see a whole new side of them.

At the end of the day, the intention, the relationship, the expectations and feedback, the coaching, the conflict management, the thoughtful onboarding—all of these things work together to ensure not only that your team members can operate at their best but also that you as a manager can too.

And that's how we make managing easier.

Conclusion

I was minding my own business, managing a team of program managers in a field that I knew inside and out, when all of a sudden my manager told me, "You're going to be managing David."

Now, I liked David; he was awesome. But David was an engineer and, as we've established, I didn't have an engineering background. What was I supposed to help him with? What use would I be to him? Would he be disappointed with this manager change?

I really worried about it, and deciding it was never going to work out, I asked my manager to rethink the decision. Three days later, I became David's manager.

In our first 1:1 meeting, I came to the conversation nervous, wondering if he was going to complain about having me as his manager. But instead, he said to me, "I'm struggling a lot with this leadership stuff. I know how to be an engineer; I don't really need help there. But where I go wrong is with influencing people and bringing visibility to my work, and I know you're great at helping people with that. That's why I'm so excited to be working for you."

It was difficult to maintain a straight face as my metaphorical jaw dropped to the floor when I realized, *Oh yeah, my job is not for me to do his job; it's to help him do his job.*

David's eagerness to work with me reenergized my intention as a manager—to help my team members get unstuck when it came to their careers—and laid a foundation of trust from the outset. I strengthened this trust by living up to my intention. We met regularly so I could learn more about where he felt like he was struggling in terms of his leadership skills, and we identified opportunities for him to showcase his work so he could start building more influence. For example, he was responsible for the IT and computer hardware on the team, and we strategized ways to showcase how his work led to cost savings, resulting in a weekly report he sent to our VP. As this report started to gain traction, I coached him on how to present the information in a way that was more digestible and how to bring a clearer narrative to the impact of the cost savings.

As David started to build more confidence in his work, his desire to build and manage a team grew. I even enlisted the help of my manager to provide David with the opportunity to mentor new folks on the team, which he found really motivating. It gave him a taste of managing even without being able to hire. But as managing was his longer-term goal, David's time on the team ultimately came to an end when he found a role at a startup where he could build an IT team from the ground up.

It was a bummer to lose such a great team member, but I was grateful that I had the opportunity to stretch all my skills as a manager and shed my initial impostor feelings around not having

Conclusion

direct experience in his role. By demonstrating genuine curiosity about what he was working on and the systems and tools he used, I was able to gain an understanding of the nature of his specific work and help him navigate challenges. And by understanding the career path he wanted to take, I could help him gain the skills he needed to grow along that path, even if that meant losing a great employee.

Working with David taught me that when we're managing, we're often our own toughest critics, deciding before we enter a situation that it's not going to work out. When we instead bring together all the tools in this book and really work at getting them right, we can help our team members reach their ultimate potential, even when the path doesn't seem clear at first.

Whether you read this book before managing your first team member, have had a few rocky starts, or are enjoying managing and really just don't want to screw it up, you're in the right place. You are committed to learning, practicing, and doing your best.

As they say about parenting, it's the people who are most concerned about messing up who are the best at it, because they're the ones who actually care.

Remember the stat that 50 percent of people have left a team because of a bad manager? By reaching the end of this book, I'm pretty damn sure you are going to be on the right side of that 50 percent.

I started the book by talking about both the power and the responsibility that come with being a manager. If the Spider-Man reference doesn't land for you, I invite you to think about yourself as a conductor in a symphony. Everyone in your orchestra has an important role to play; no one is redundant. Each person is incredibly talented on their own, but when they come together—with the right guidance and expectations set around timing and flow—they make the most beautiful music.

This book is intended to be a crash course in the foundational skills you need to develop to be an effective manager, and my hope is that in reading it, you feel more confident in your role.

My mission is to make managing the easiest part of people's jobs. Hopefully your next feedback conversation, 1:1, performance review—or you name it—will be just a little bit easier.

Investing the time in reading, getting coaching and mentorship, and attending trainings or workshops your company hosts will help you shorten the learning curve so your job can get easier faster.

Keep practicing.

This is called a playbook for a reason. Come back to it as a reference: do the exercises, use the tools, and download the worksheets. Sooner than you think, all these skills will start to click.

There will always be good days and bad days, but you will have fewer bad ones when your team members feel you are invested in them as people and that you see your role as helping them be successful.

Conclusion

With your intention set and a commitment to following through, you are going to crush this manager thing.

And if you get stuck along the way, I hope you now see that you don't have to muscle through it alone.

Here are a few ways to get more support:

- Download the resources and exercises shared in this book at liagarvin.com/playbook-resources.
- Reach out at liagarvin.com/signup for 1:1 coaching, interactive workshops for your team, or manager development trainings for your company, in which I bring the contents of this book to life.
- Sign up for my newsletter at liagarvin.com to keep up to date with my latest podcast episodes, learn about new workshops and programs, and receive more tips and tools.
- Subscribe to my podcast *Managing Made Simple* on Spotify or Apple, where every Tuesday I share tools, tips, and stories to make managing easier.
- Follow me on Instagram and YouTube: @lia.garvin.
- Connect with me on LinkedIn: linkedin.com/in/liagarvin.

Don't be a stranger!

Acknowledgments

Thank you to the managers throughout my career who believed in me, helped me stretch in new ways, and taught me to believe in myself. I've been blessed to work for some truly amazing people, and without what I learned from them, I would not be helping others become great managers today. Thank you, David Winter, Graeme Muirhead, Ben Pham, Albert Shum, Michael Smuga, James Fiduccia, Jon Wiley, Rachel Smith, and Elizabeth Belg.

Thank you to my family and friends for your support and belief—and for encouraging me to keep doing what I do every single day.

Thank you to my incredible editors, Anastasia Voll and Courtney Kerrigan, who completely got the concept from the first moment and ensured everything was clear, easy to read, and actionable. You made writing this book a joy, and I am so grateful for the time and care you took with this book.

Thank you to Jake Kelfer, Mikey Kershisnik, and then entire team at Big Idea to Bestseller for continually over-delivering and bringing this book to life.

Thank you to the entrepreneur community that I have built up since leaving the corporate world. Running a business is as terrifying and overwhelming as it is exhilarating and exciting, and each and every one of you has been invaluable to me to lean on and bounce ideas off of. You inspire me to keep going. Thank you, Cristina Gordon, Chris Hader, Kristina Bartold-Sorgota, Staci Millard, Jackie Koch, Andy and Meghan Clor, Cory Charles, Shaun Peet, Meghan Houle, Kerri Jacobs, Mike LeMieux, Rashae Doyle, and Monica Boudreau, among many, many others.

Thank you to my clients who have entrusted me with their leadership journey and helping them build their best possible team.

Thank you to all of my *Managing Made Simple* podcast listeners who support the show. From folks sharing it with their teams to listening with their colleagues, I could not be more grateful to hear all of the ways the show has helped you be better leaders and feel less overwhelmed as managers.

And thank YOU, reader, for taking this step to become a great manager. Keep showing up and it *will* get easier.

Help spread the word!

If you enjoyed the book, please take two minutes to leave a quick review wherever you purchased the book!

Reviews spread the word about the book and help make managing easier for more folks out there. Let's face it: no matter the industry, the better managers there are, the better the work done by their teams will be—and we all benefit.

Thank you in advance for your support!

Endnotes

1. Marcus Buckingham and Curt Coffman, *First, Break All the Rules: What the World's Greatest Managers Do Differently* (New York: Simon & Schuster, 1999), 31.

2. Tim Nolan, "The No. 1 Employee Benefit That No One's Talking About," *Workplace* (blog), Gallup, Oct. 12, 2017, https://www.gallup.com/workplace/232955/no-employee-benefit-no-one-talking.aspx.

3. Dawn Klinghoffer and Katie Kirkpatrick-Husk, "With Burnout on the Rise, What Can Companies Do About It?," *MIT Sloan Management Review*, May 12, 2023, https://sloanreview.mit.edu/article/with-burnout-on-the-rise-what-can-companies-do-about-it/.

4. M.T. O'Neill, V. Jones, and A. Reid, "Impact of Menopausal Symptoms on Work and Careers: A Cross-Sectional Study," *Occupational Medicine* 73, no. 6 (August 2023): 332-338, https://doi.org/10.1093/occmed/kqad078.

5. Erin Meyer, *The Culture Map: Breaking Through the Invisible Boundaries of Global Business* (New York: PublicAffairs, 2014).

6. Erica Dhawan, *Digital Body Language: How to Build Trust and Connection, No Matter the Distance* (New York, St. Martin's Press, 2021).

7. Gallup, Inc., *State of the American Manager: Analytics and Advice for Leaders,* April 7, 2015, https://www.gallup.com/services/182138/state-american-manager.aspx.

8. Daniel Coyle, *The Culture Code: The Secrets of Highly Successful Groups* (New York: Bantam Books, 2018).

9. "John Wooden," *Encyclopedia Britannica,* last modified Oct. 10, 2024, https://www.britannica.com/biography/John-Wooden.

10. Bas Verplanken and Suzanne Faes, "Good Intentions, Bad Habits, and Effects of Forming Implementation Intentions on Healthy Eating," *European Journal of Social Psychology* 29 no. 5–6 (June 21, 1999): 591–604, https://doi.org/10.1002/(SICI)1099-0992(199908/09)29:5/6<591::AID-EJSP948>3.0.CO;2-H.

11. Stephen R. Covey, *The 7 Habits of Highly Effective People: Restoring the Character Ethic,* rev. ed. (New York: Free Press, 2004).

12. Paul J. Zak, "The Neuroscience of Trust," *Harvard Business Review,* January – February 2017, https://hbr.org/2017/01/the-neuroscience-of-trust.

13. Dana Brownlee, "5 Reasons Why Trust Matters on Teams," *Forbes,* Oct. 20, 2019, https://www.forbes.com/sites/danabrownlee/2019/10/20/5-reasons-why-trust-matters-on-teams/.

14. Amy C. Edmondson, "Leading in Tough Times," *Recruiting: Insights & Advice* (blog), Harvard Business School, Nov. 22, 2022, https://www.hbs.edu/recruiting/insights-and-advice/blog/post/leading-in-tough-times.

15. Charles Duhigg, "What Google Learned From Its Quest to Build the Perfect Team," *The New York Times Magazine,* Feb. 25, 2016, https://www.nytimes.com/2016/02/28/magazine/what-google-learned-from-its-quest-to-build-the-perfect-team.html.

16. Patrick Lencioni, The Advantage: Why Organizational Health Trumps Everything Else in Business (San Francisco: Jossey-Bass, 2012), 28.

17. Brian Armstrong, "*Coinbase Is a Mission Focused Company*" (blog), Coinbase, Sept. 27, 2020, https://www.coinbase.com/blog/coinbase-is-a-mission-focused-company.

18. Nicole Torres, "It's Better to Avoid a Toxic Employee than Hire a Superstar," *Harvard Business Review*, Dec. 9, 2015, https://hbr.org/2015/12/its-better-to-avoid-a-toxic-employee-than-hire-a-superstar.

19. Will Guidara, *Unreasonable Hospitality: The Remarkable Power of Giving People More than They Expect* (New York:Optimism Press, 2022), 69.

20. Elise Paulsen, "The Best One-on-One Meeting Frequency According to Research," *Quantum Workplace,* March 29, 2022, https://www.quantumworkplace.com/future-of-work/one-on-one-meeting-frequency.

21. The Grossman Group, *Burned Out & Checked Out: What Employees & Managers Need to Thrive* (white paper), April 10, 2024, https://www.yourthoughtpartner.com/hubfs/pdf/Well-Being_Research_White_Paper_Burned_Out_Checked_Out_FINAL_04102024_The_Grossman_Group.pdf.

22. Corey Tatel and Ben Weiger, "42% of Employee Turnover Is Preventable but Often Ignored," *Workplace*, Gallup, July 10, 2024, https://www.gallup.com/workplace/646538/employee-turnover-preventable-often-ignored.aspx.

23. Ben Wigert and Heather Barrett, "2% of CHROs Think Their Performance Management System Works," Workplace, Gallup, March 28, 2023, https://www.gallup.com/workplace/644717/chros-think-performance-management-system-works.aspx.

24. Douglas Stone and Sheila Heen, *Thanks for the Feedback: The Science and Art of Receiving Feedback Well (Even When It Is Off Base, Unfair, Poorly Delivered, and Frankly, You're Not in the Mood)* (New York: Viking, 2014).

25. Shanita Williams, "Why You Should Use a Strainer Instead of a Sponge to Process Feedback," TEDx Talk, Manchester, NH, Oct. 4, 2018, 14 min., 18 sec., https://www.ted.com/talks/shanita_williams_why_you_should_use_a_strainer_instead_of_a_sponge_to_process_feedback?subtitle=en.

26. Center for Creative Leadership, "Improve Talent Development with Our SBI Feedback Model," Nov. 24, 2022,https://www.ccl.org/articles/leading-effectively-articles/sbi-feedback-model-a-quick-win-to-improve-talent-conversations-development/.

27. Gallup, "The Importance of Employee Recognition: Low Cost, High Impact," Jan. 12, 2024, https://www.gallup.com/workplace/236441/employee-recognition-low-cost-high-impact.aspx.

28. Theresa Agovino, "The Power of 'Thank You,'" SHRM, Sept. 6, 2024, https://www.shrm.org/topics-tools/news/hr-quarterly/the-power-of-thank-you-.

29. Jack Zenger and Joseph Folkman, "The Ideal Praise-to-Criticism Ratio," *Harvard Business Review,* March 15, 2013, https://hbr.org/3 2013/0/the-ideal-praise-to-criticism.

30. Lia Garvin, *Unstuck: Reframe Your Thinking to Free Yourself from the Patterns and People That Hold You Back* (New York: Media Lab Books, 2022), 190.

31. Leslie A. Perlow, Constance Noonan Hadley, and Eunice Eun, "Stop the Meeting Madness: How to Free Up Time for Meaningful Work," *Harvard Business Review*, July–August 2017, https://hbr.org/2017/07/stop-the-meeting-madness.

32. Jocelyne Gafner, "The Impact of Workplace Wellbeing and How to Foster It," *Indeed Career Guide*, Aug. 18, 2024, https://www.indeed.com/career-advice/career-development/workplace-wellbeing.

33. Everything DiSC, "Human Connection: The Crucial Secret to Thriving in the Digital Age," *Wiley Workplace Intelligence*, May 24, 2024, https://www.everythingdisc.com/blogs/human-connection-the-crucial-secret-to-thriving-in-the-digital-age/.

34. Lori Harder, host, *Earn Your Happy*, podcast, "How to Build and Manage a Winning Team with HR Expert Jackie Koch," September 16, 2024, https://podcasts.apple.com/us/podcast/how-to-build-and-manage-a-winning-team-with-hr/id1087926635?i=1000669687403.

35. Diana Hill, "What Is Non-Attachment and Why You Should Be Practicing It" (blog), *Insight Timer*, accessed Sept. 29, 2024, https://insighttimer.com/blog/what-is-non-attachment-and-why-you-should-be-practicing-it/.

36. Roy Maurer, "Onboarding Key to Retaining, Engaging Talent," *SHRM*, April 16, 2015, https://www.shrm.org/resourcesandtools/hr-topics/talent-acquisition/pages/onboarding-key-retaining-engaging-talent.aspx.

37. James Dunne, "Can Better Tech Really Fix Darker-Skin Bias in Smartphone Cameras? Google Thinks So," *CBC News*, Feb. 27, 2022, https://www.cbc.ca/news/business/google-real-tone-pixel-1.6363809.

38. Sasha Rogelberg, "Chanel's CEO Went to Microsoft HQ and Asked ChatGPT to Show Her a Picture of Her Company's Leadership. They Were All Men in Suits," *Fortune*, Oct. 30, 2024, https://fortune.com/-2024/10/30/chanel-ceo-leena-nair-microsoft-openai-chatgpt/.

39. HRbrain.ai, "DEI Biases in Job Descriptions: Best Practices," Jan. 26, 2024, https://hrbrain.ai/blog/dei-biases-in-job-descriptions-best-practices/.